AF378542

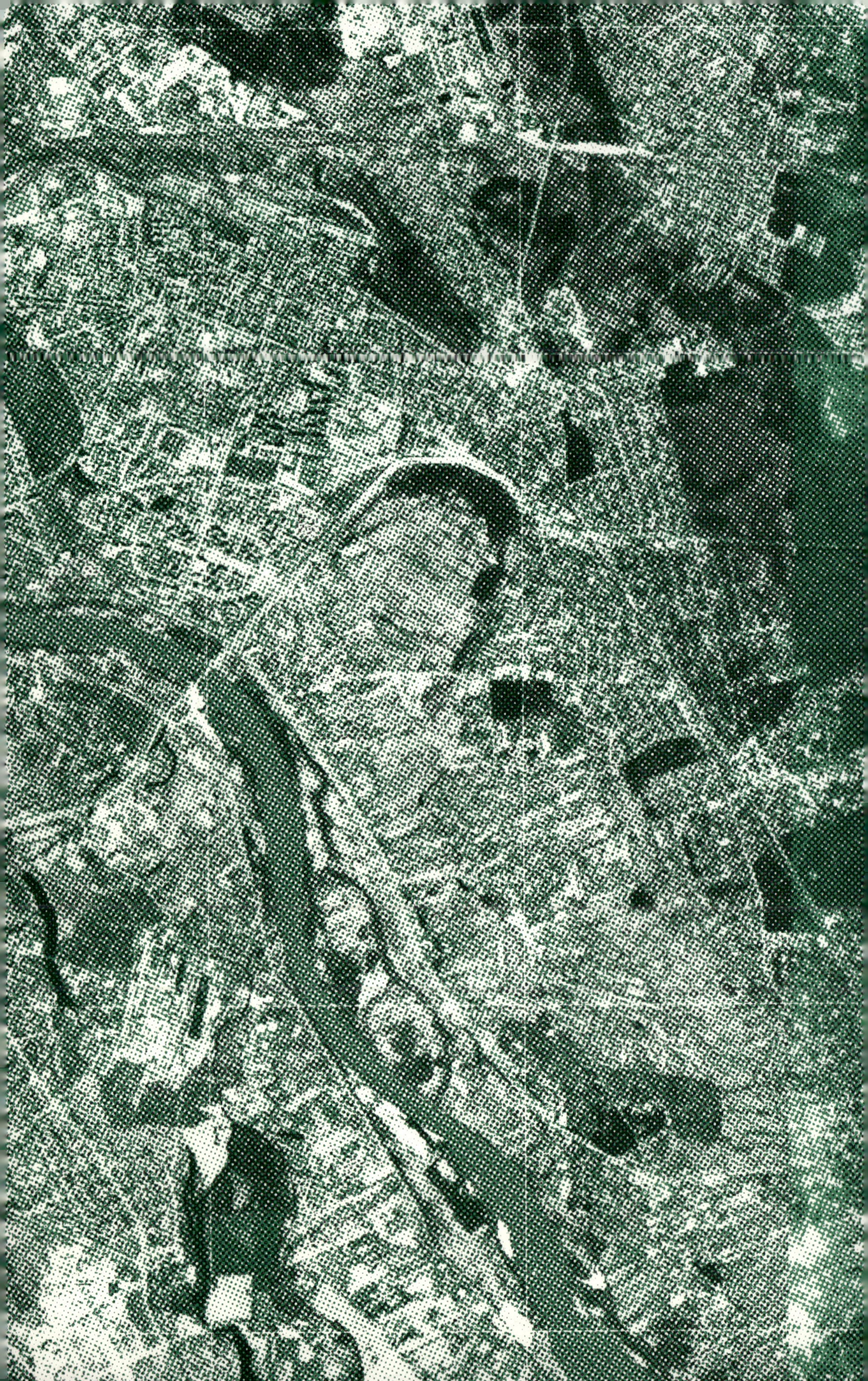

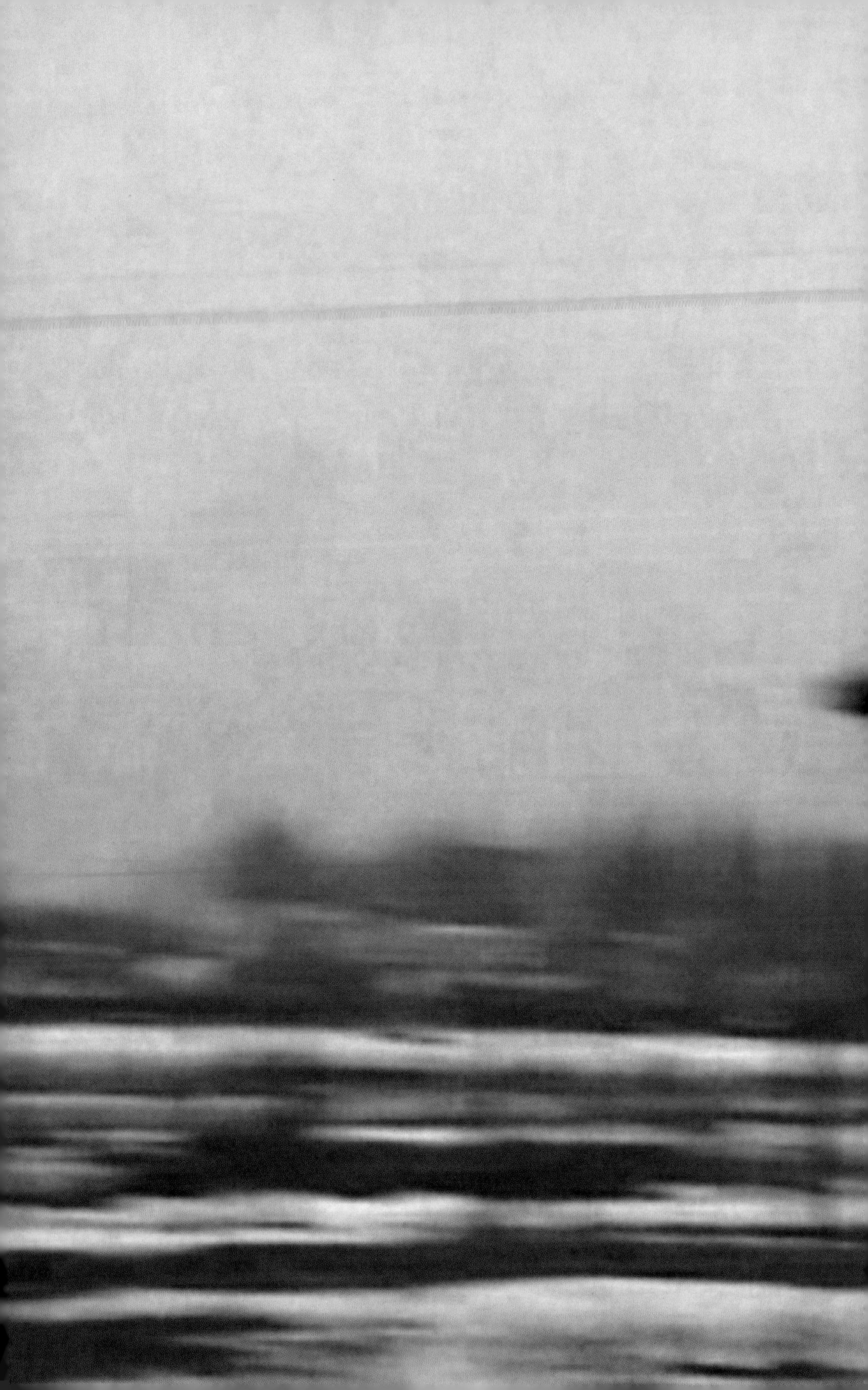

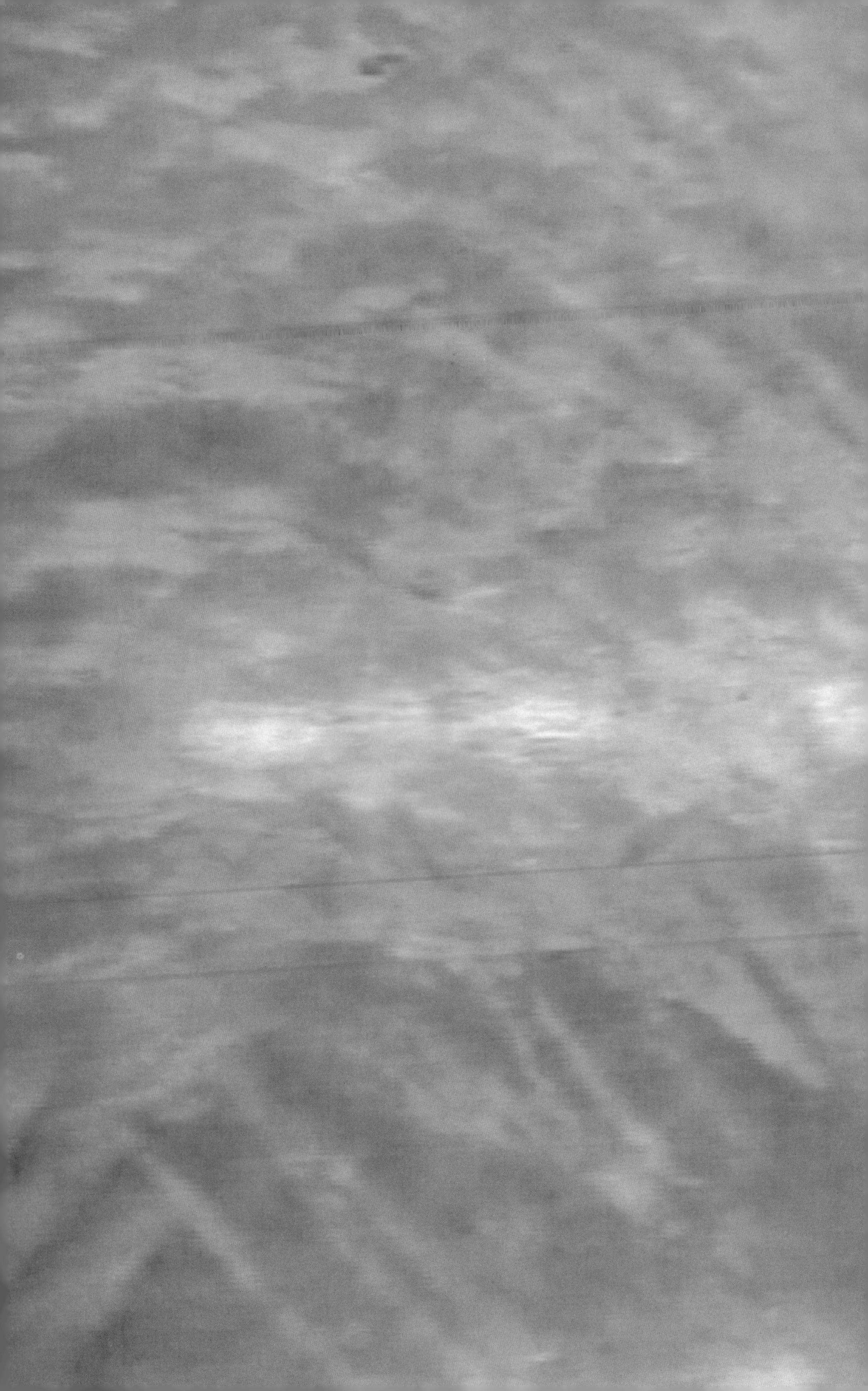

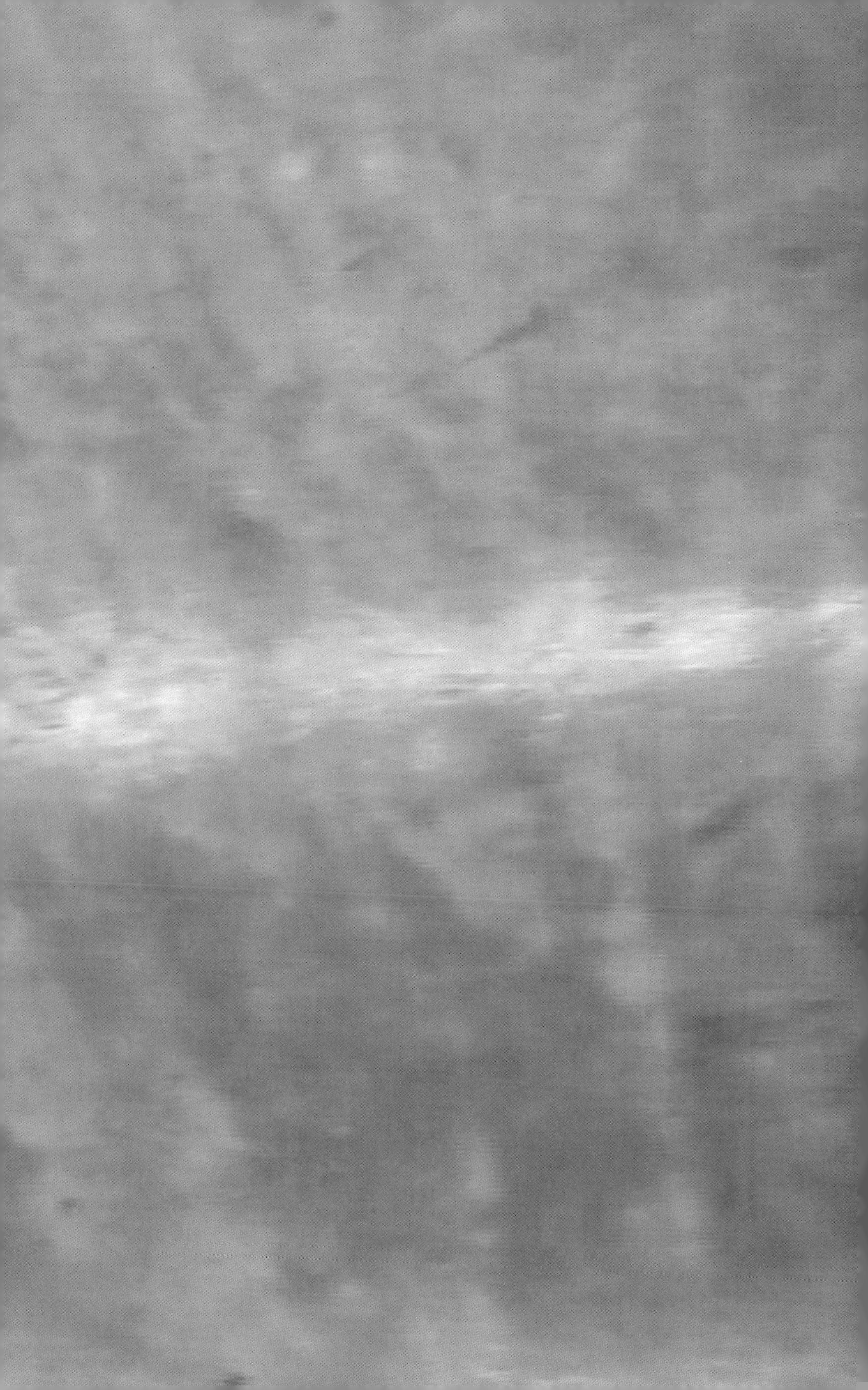

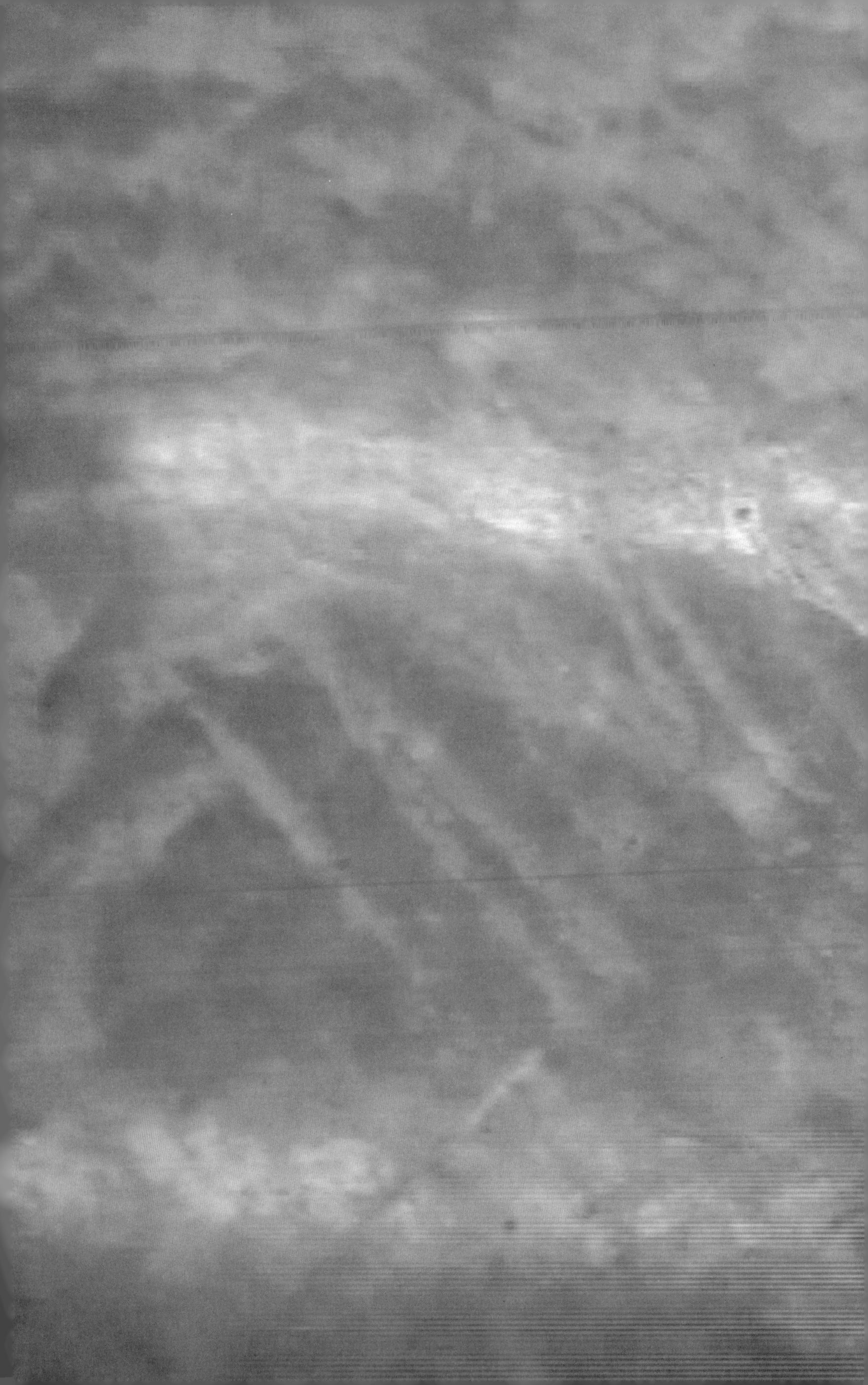

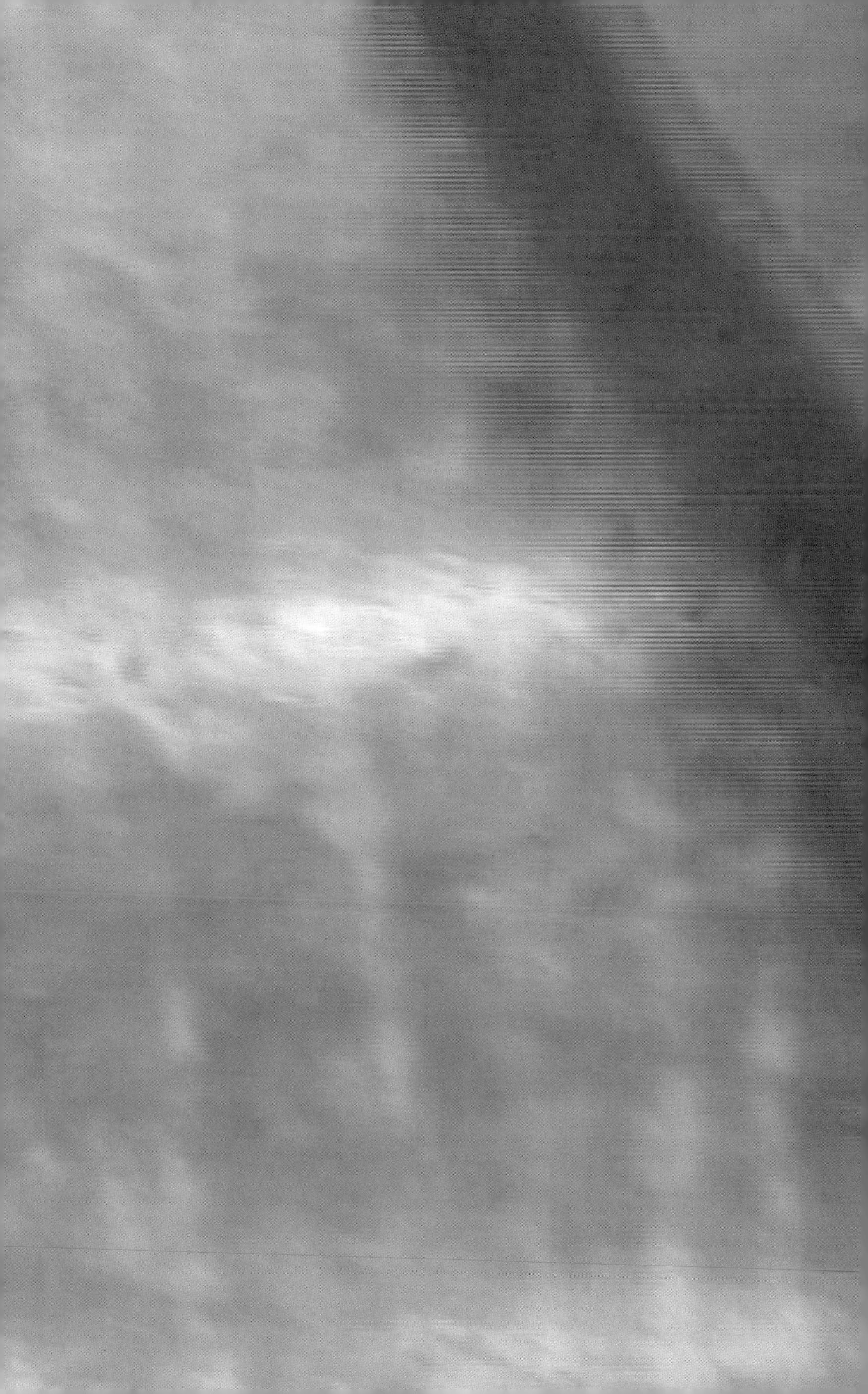

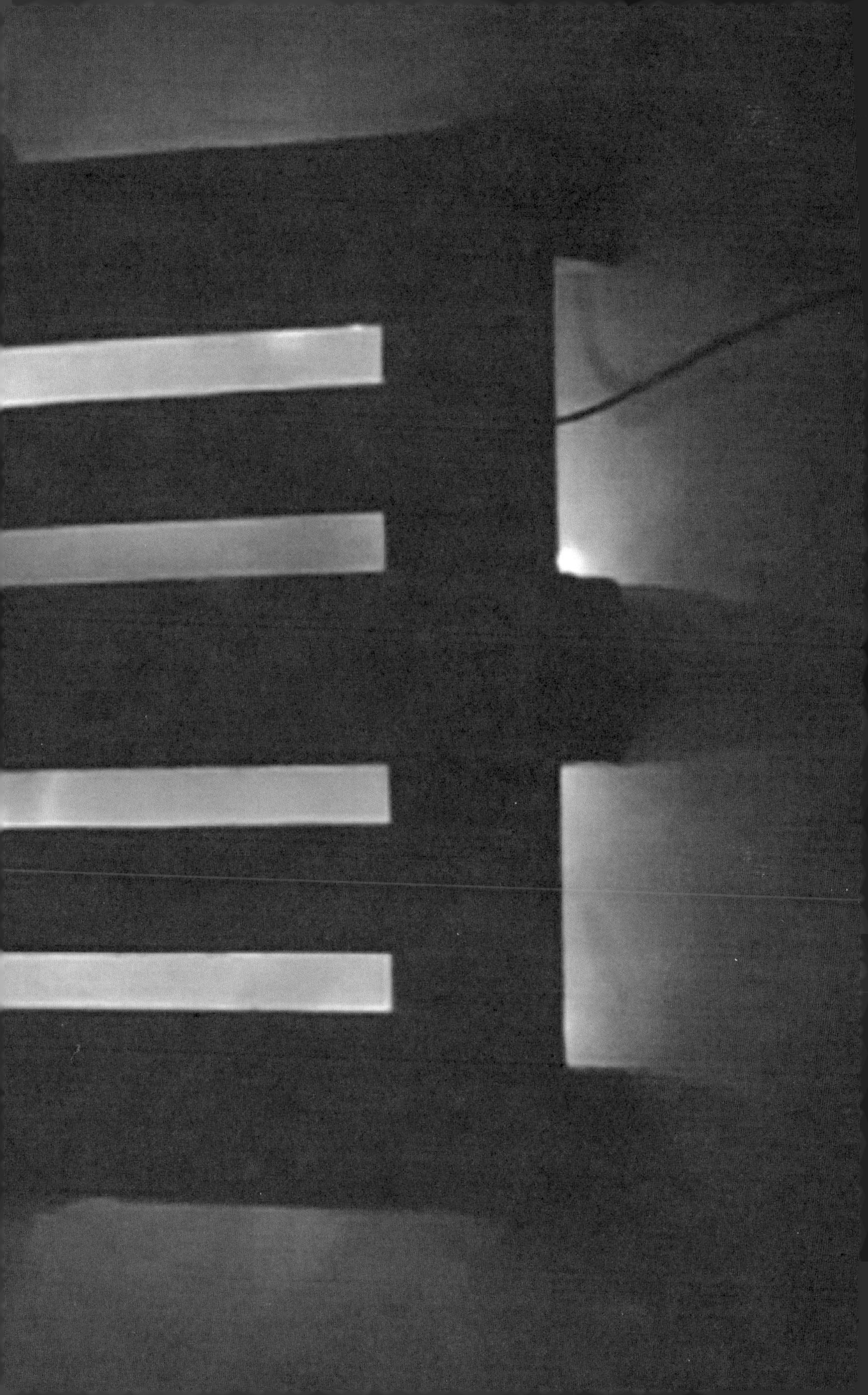

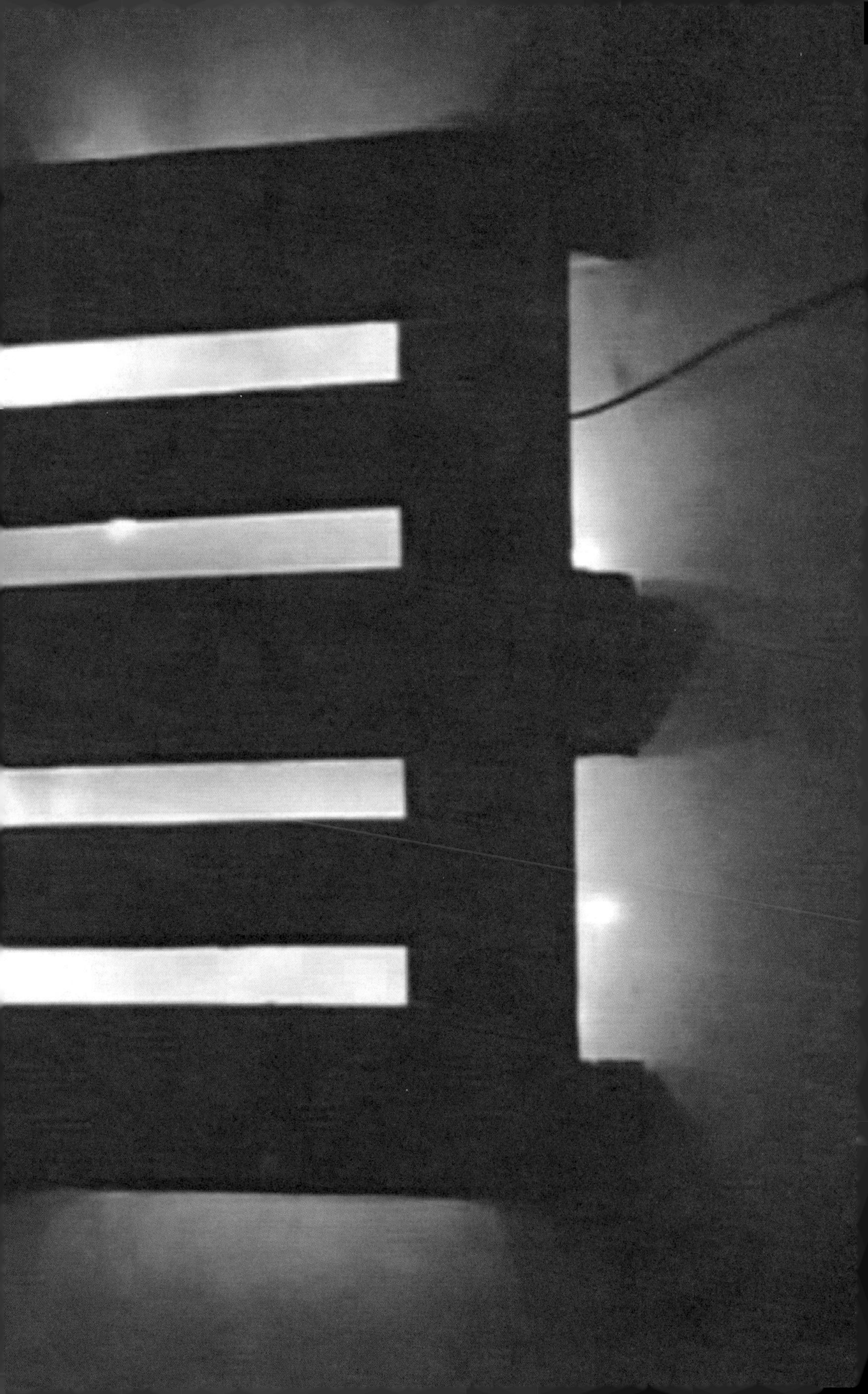

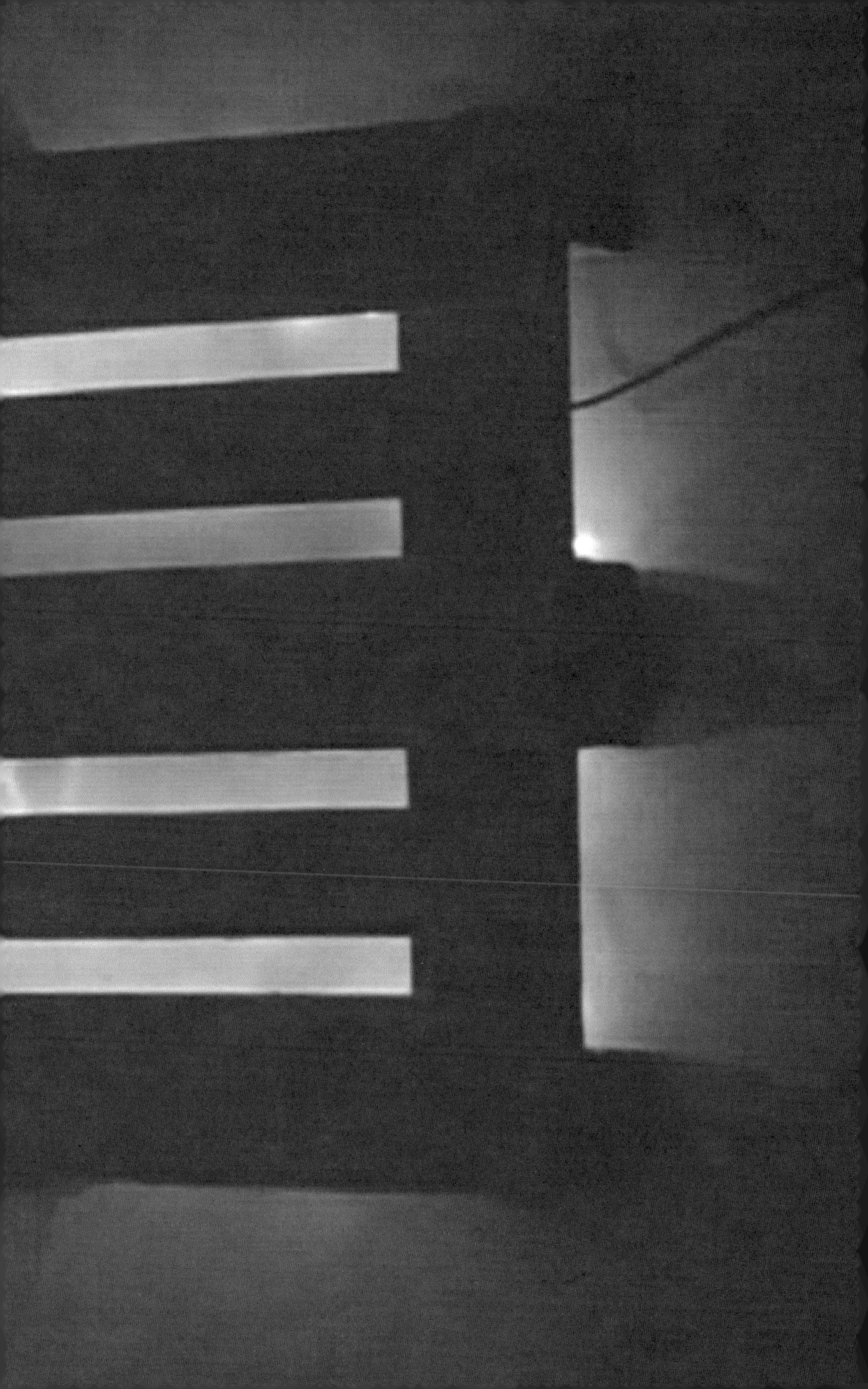

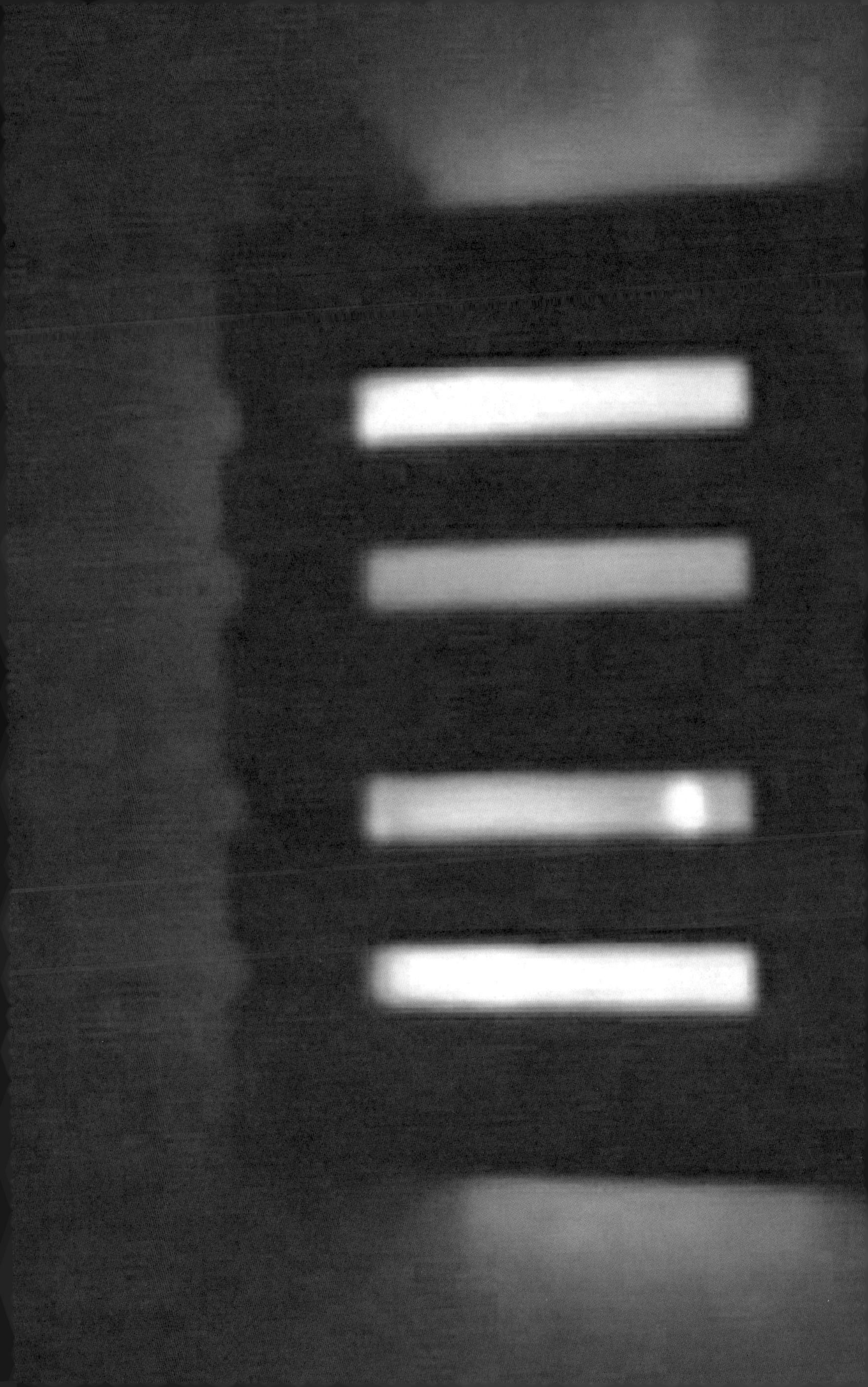

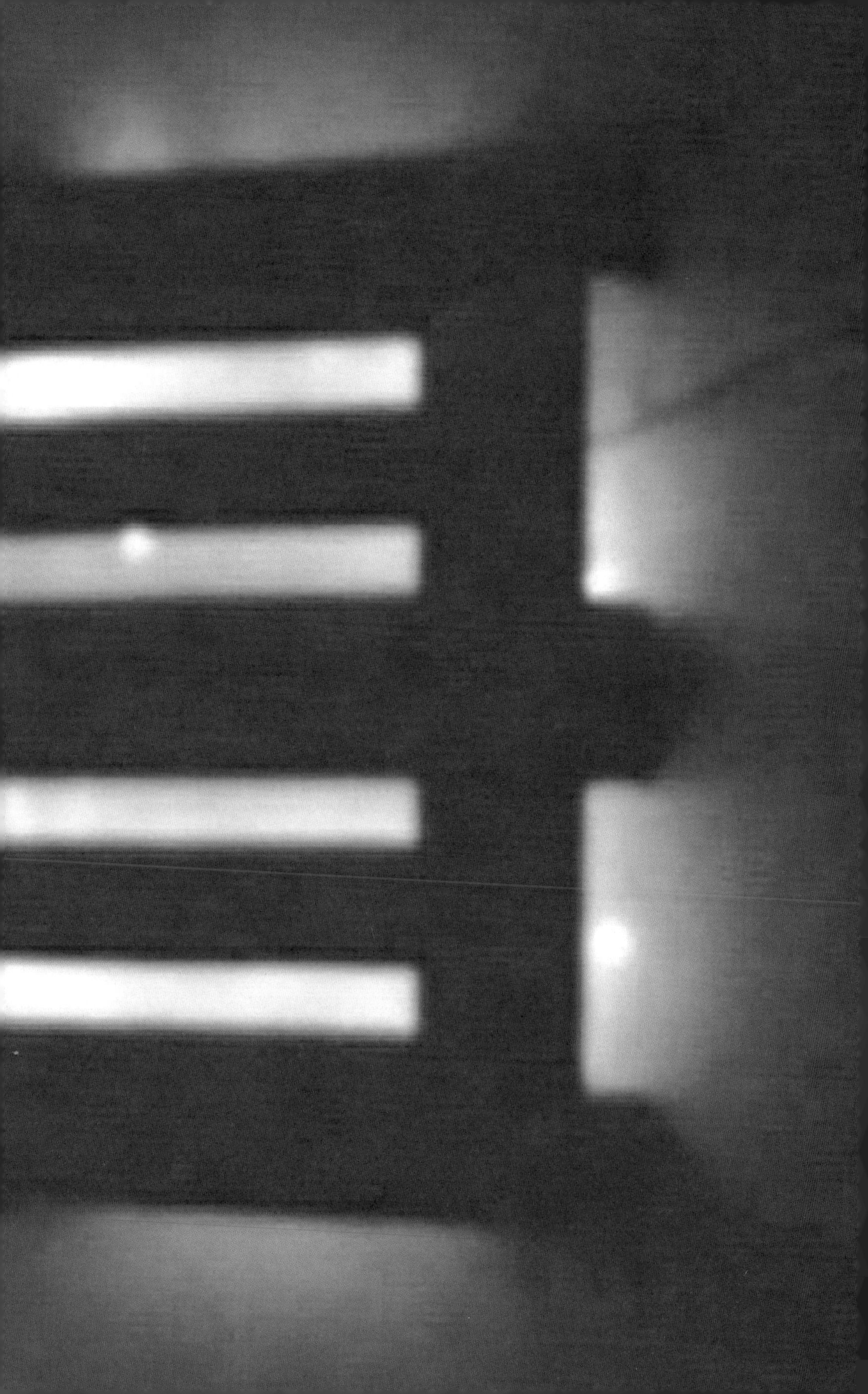

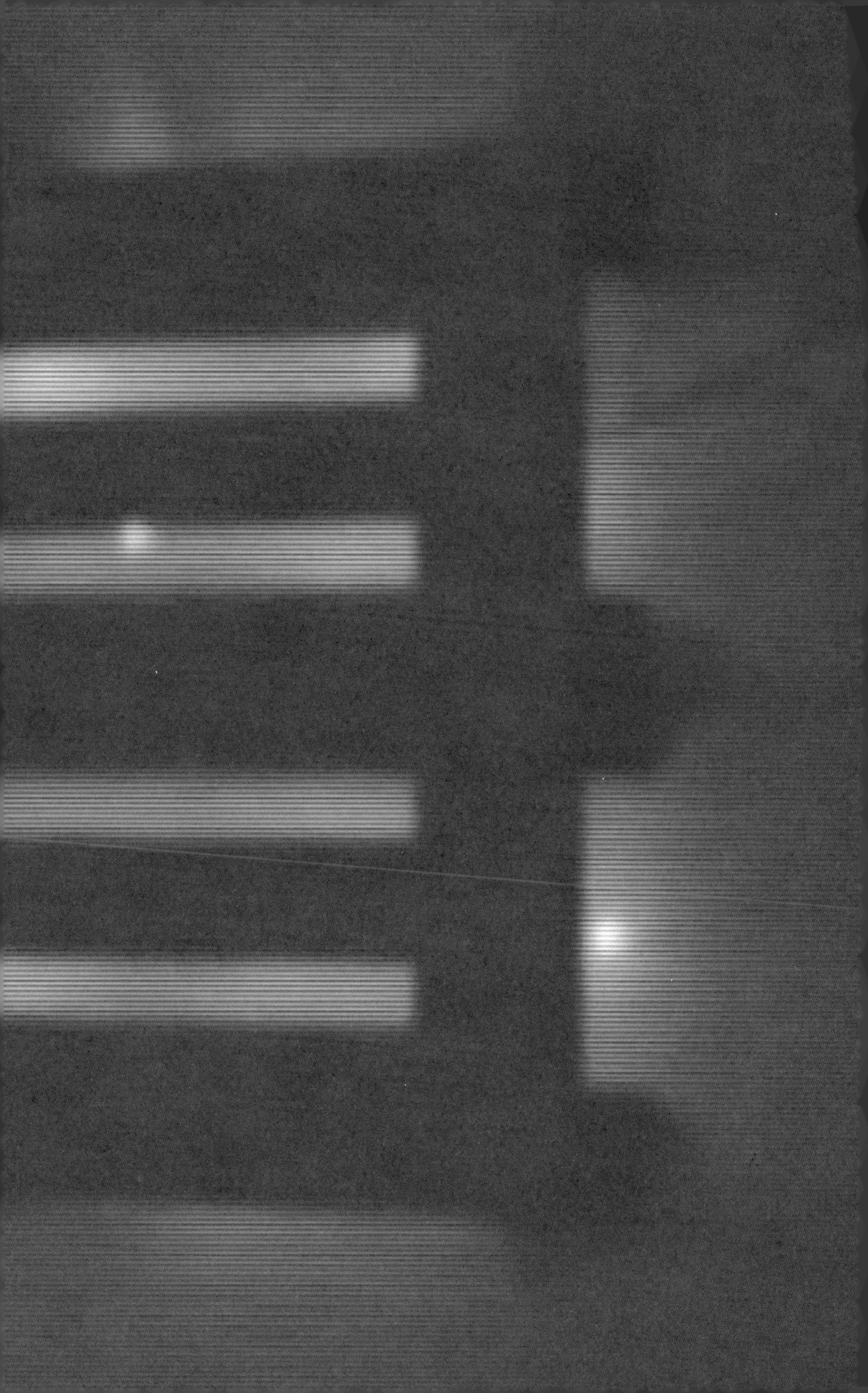

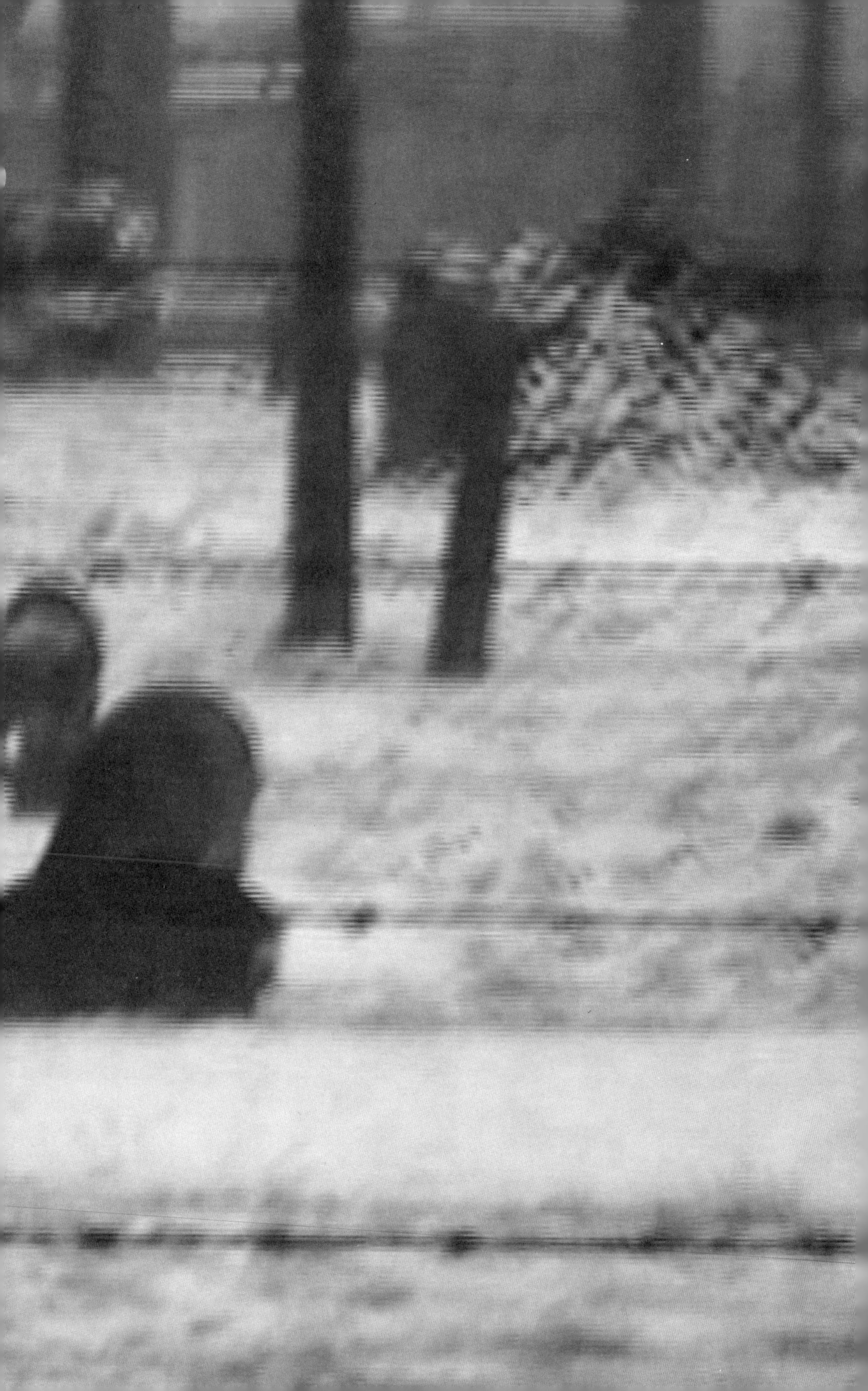

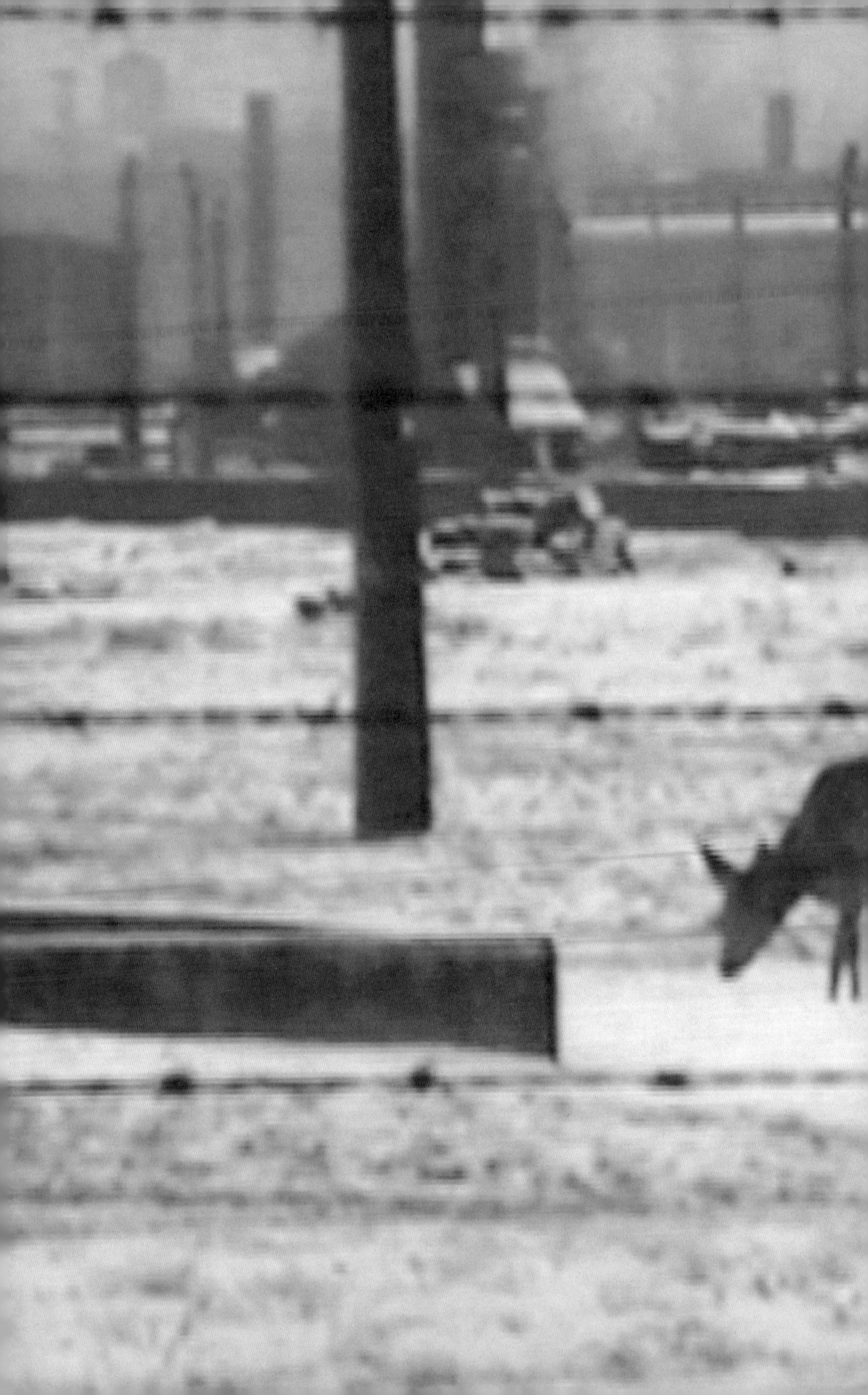

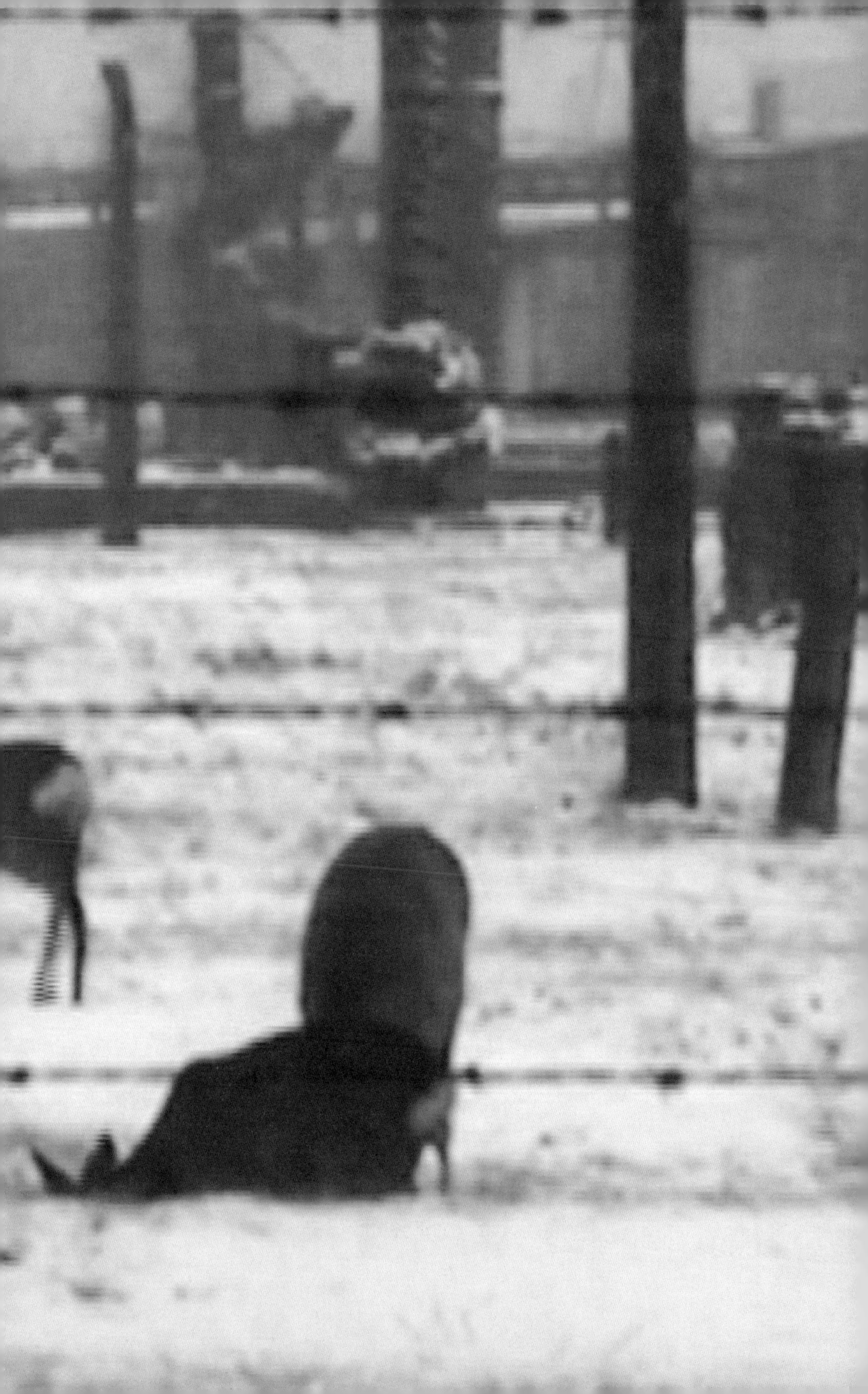

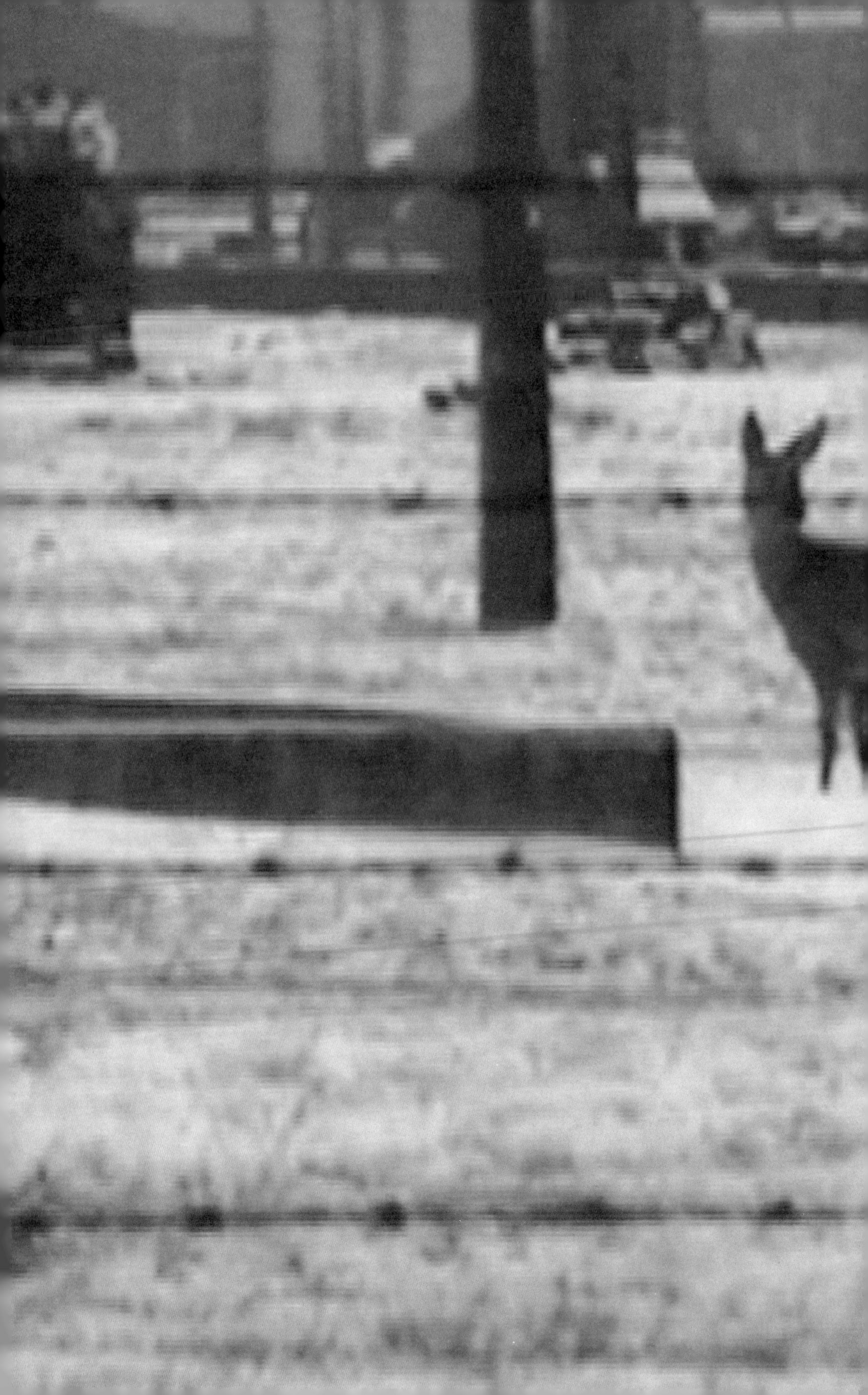

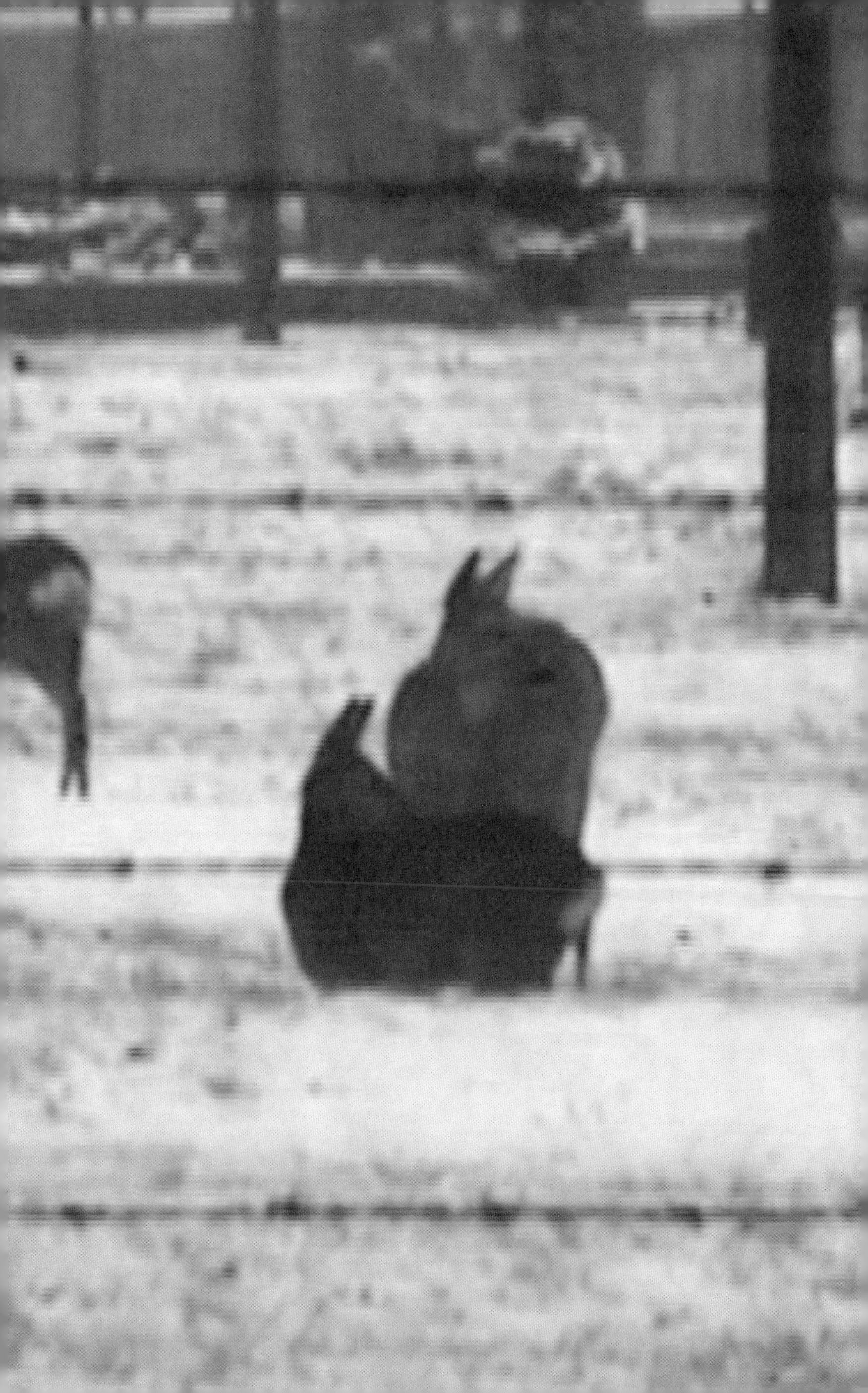

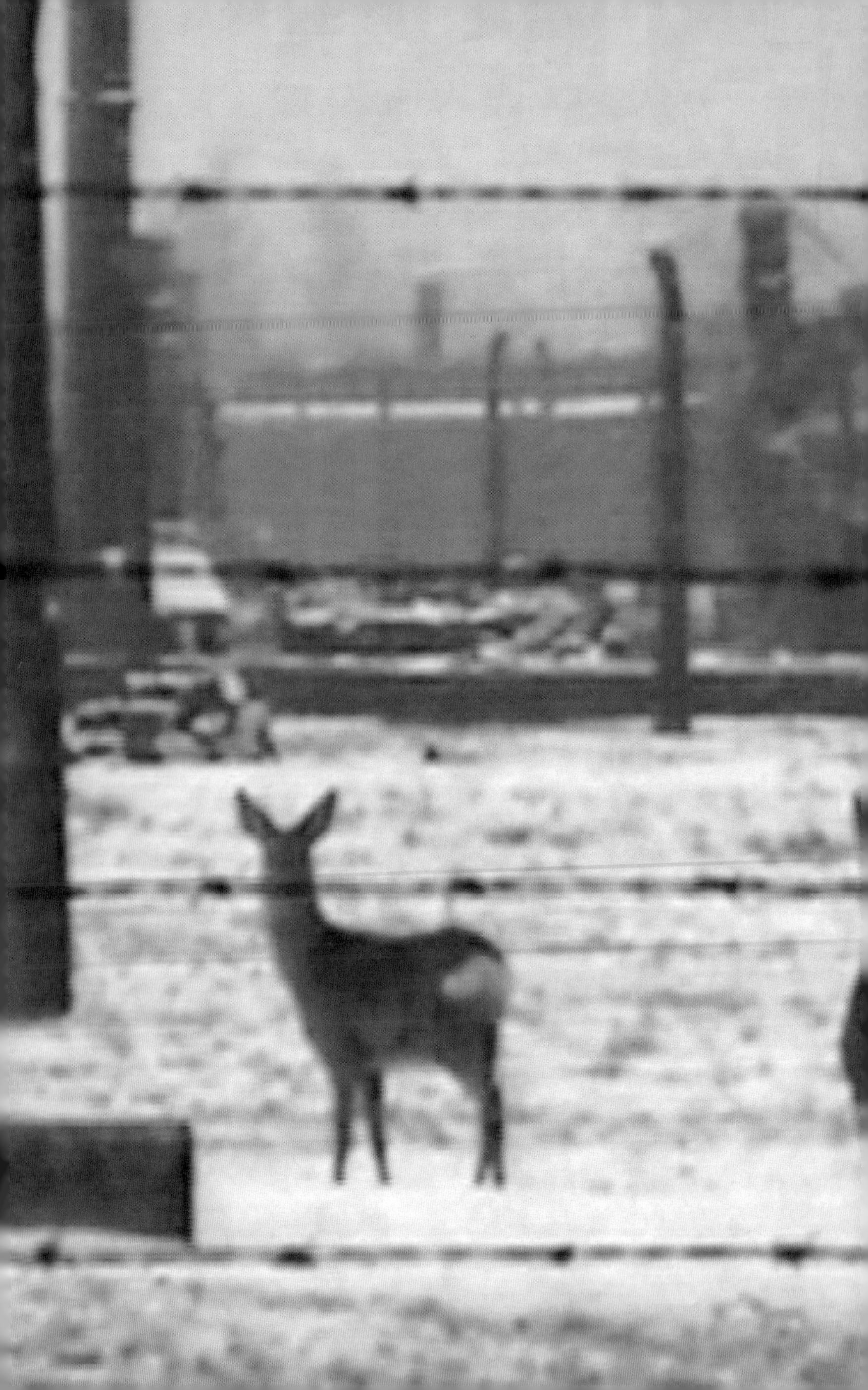

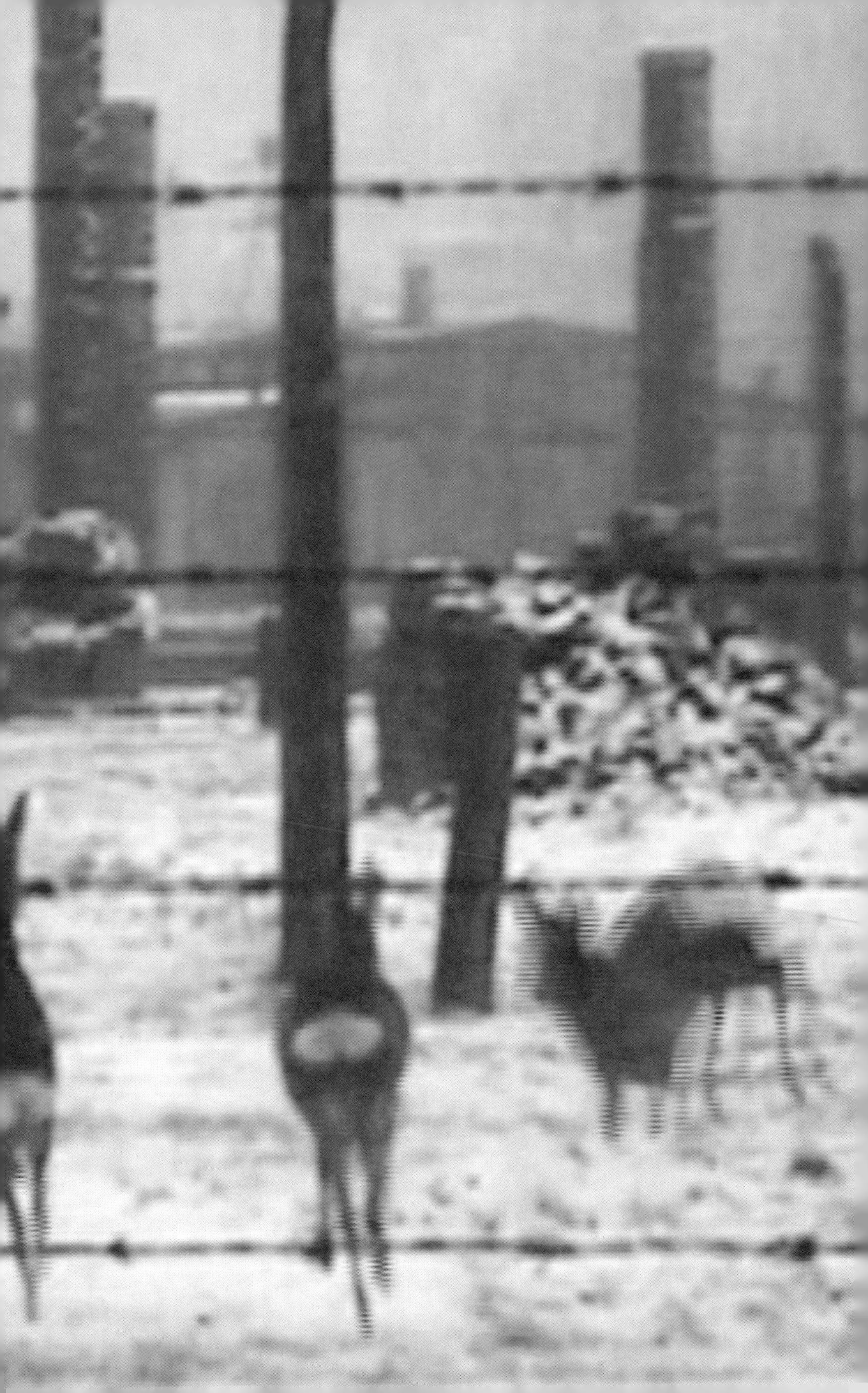

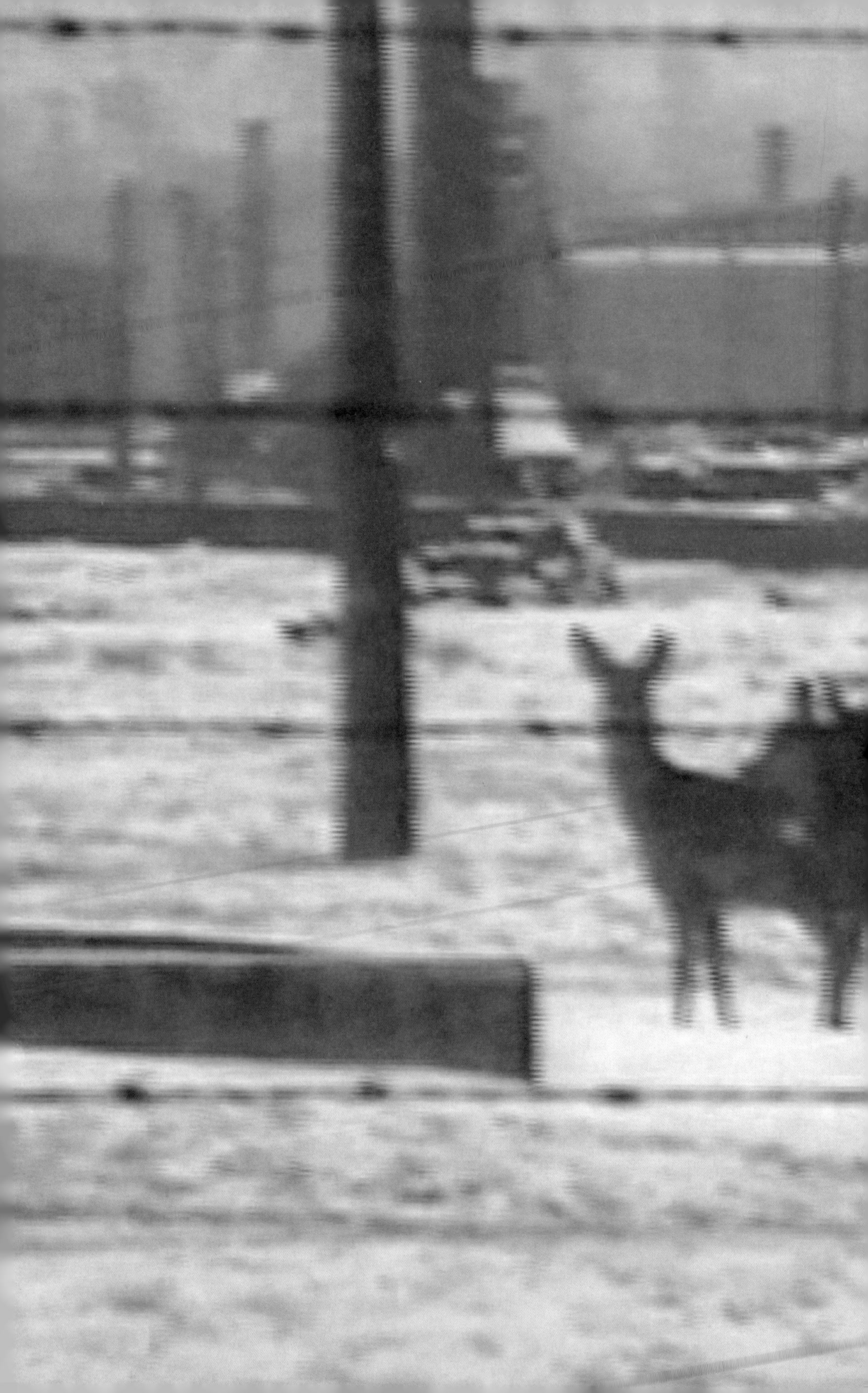

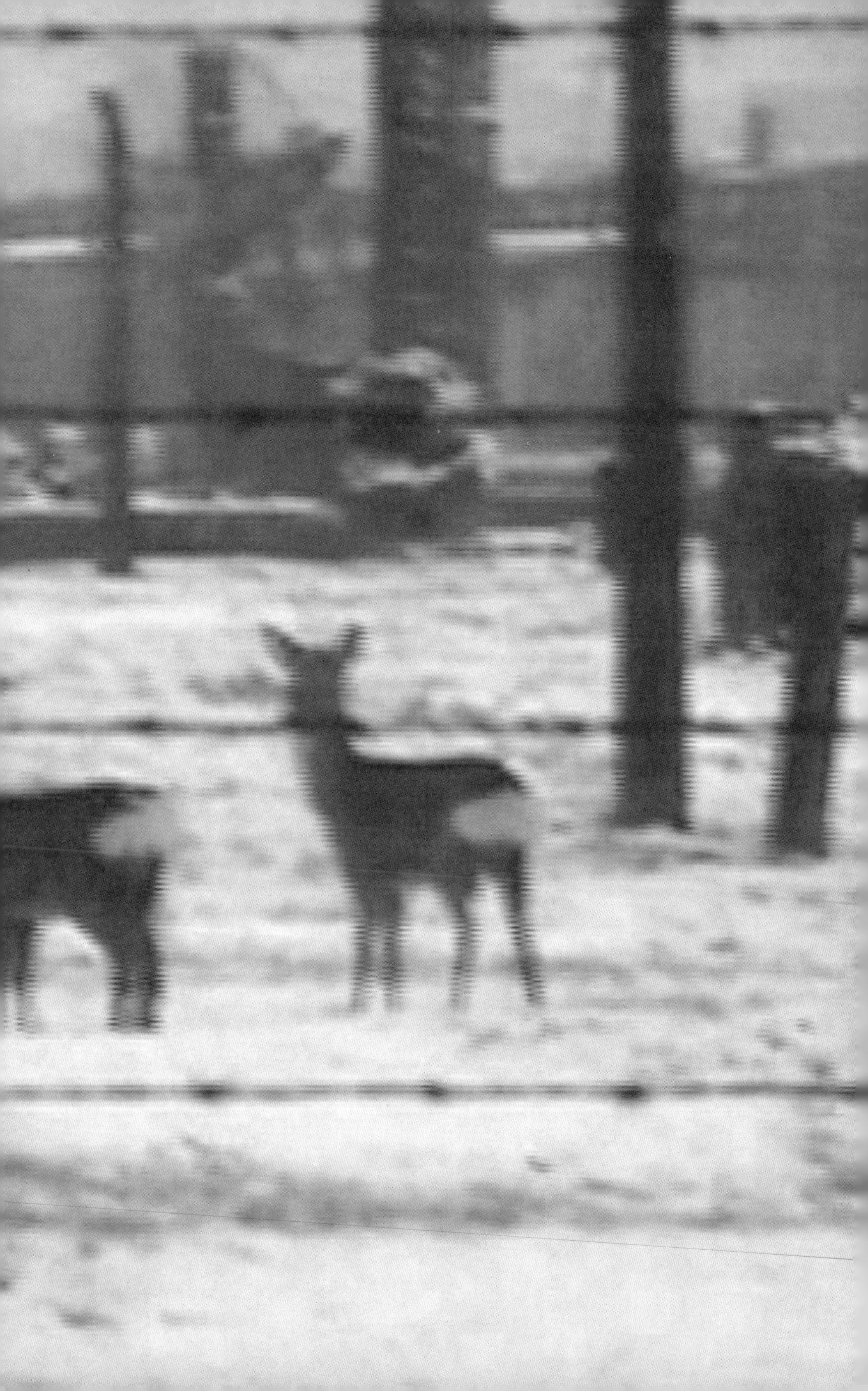

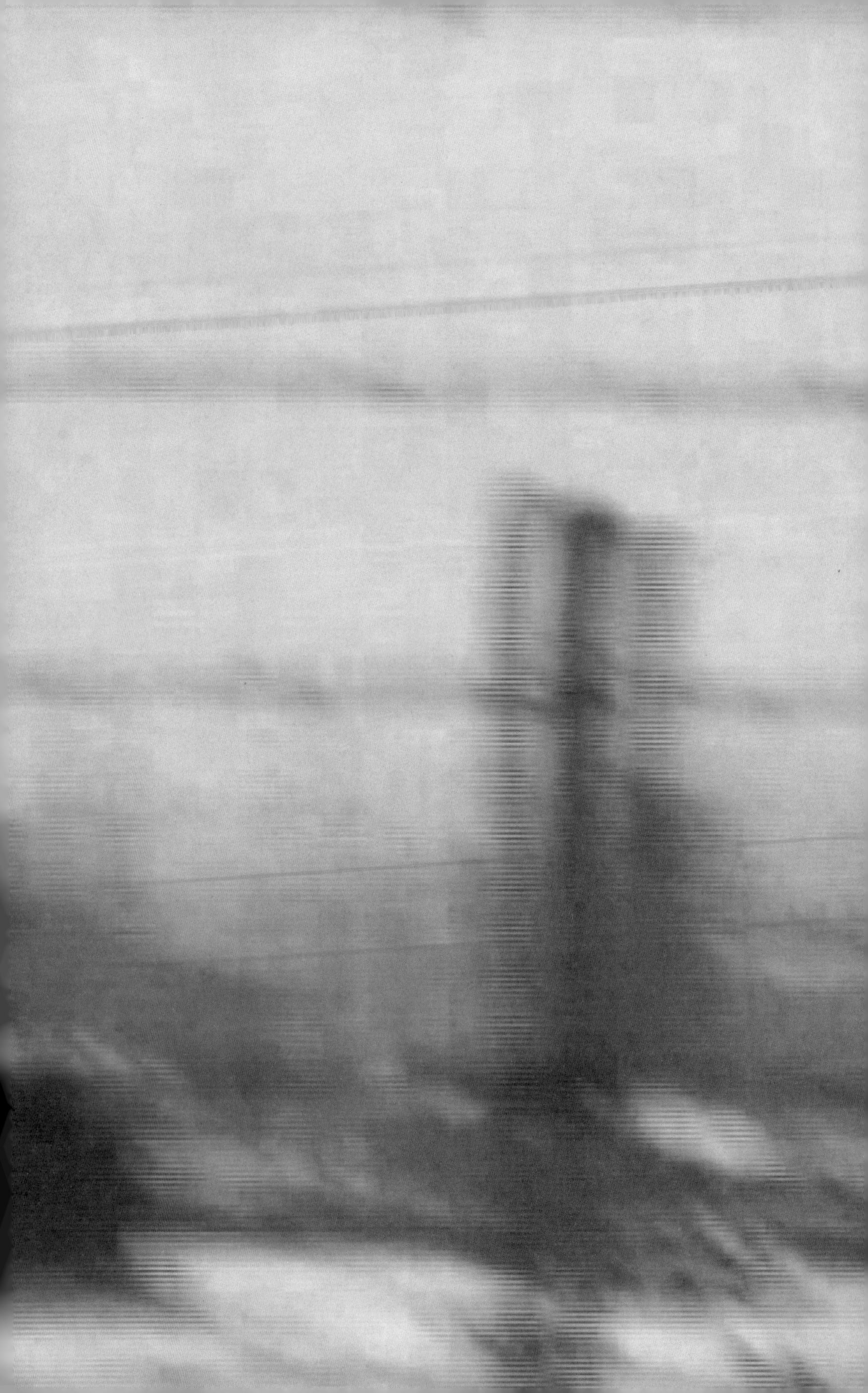

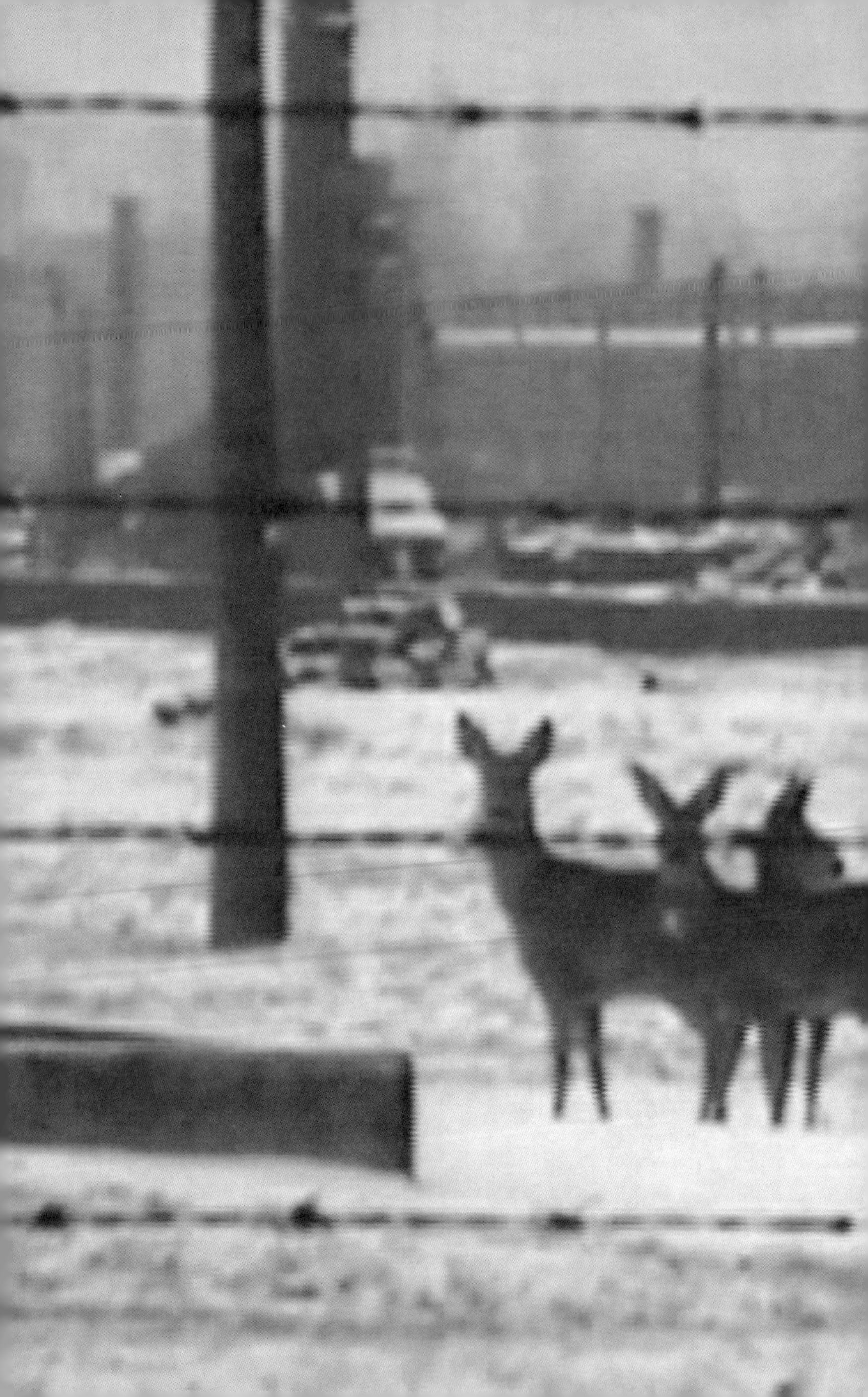

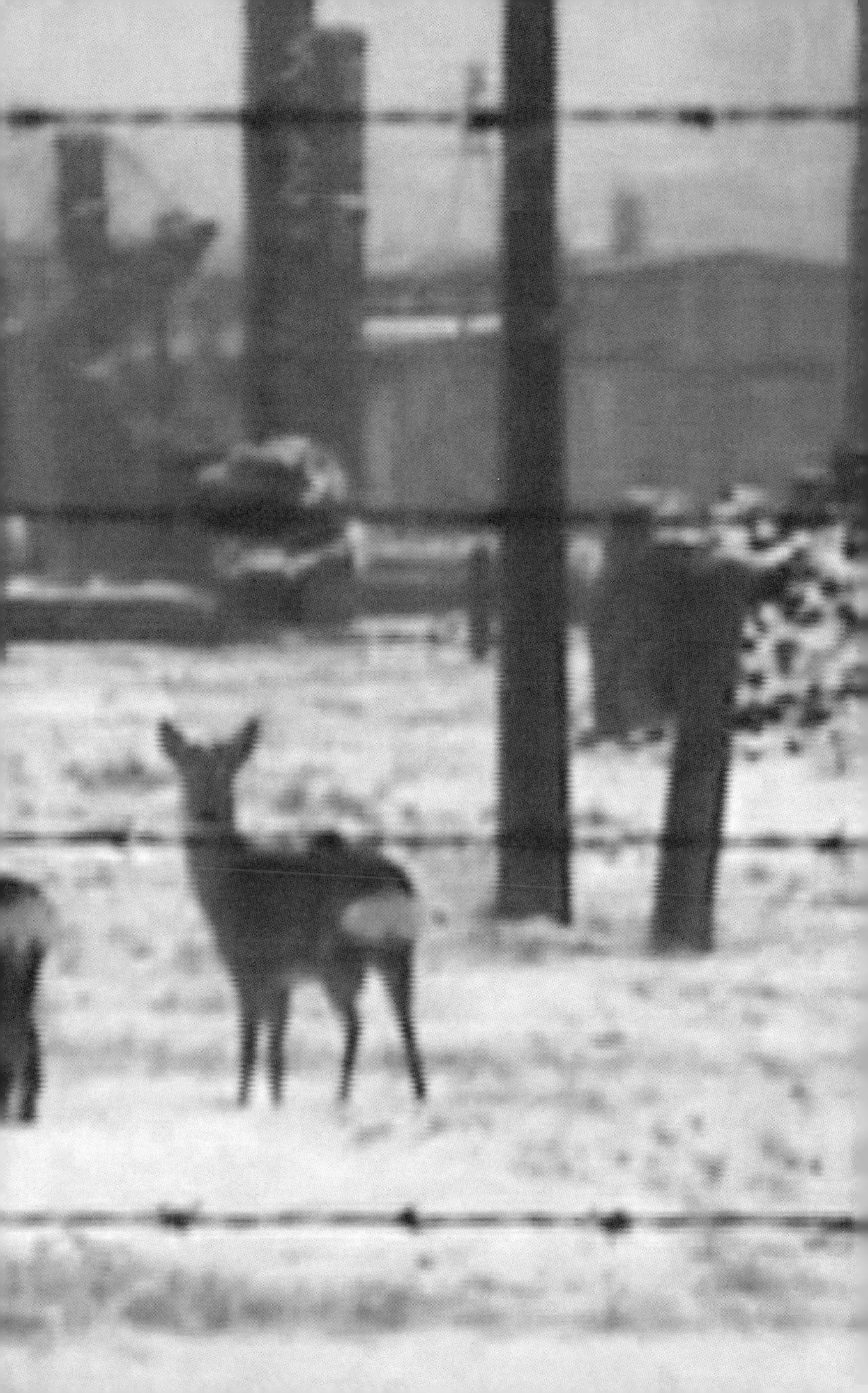

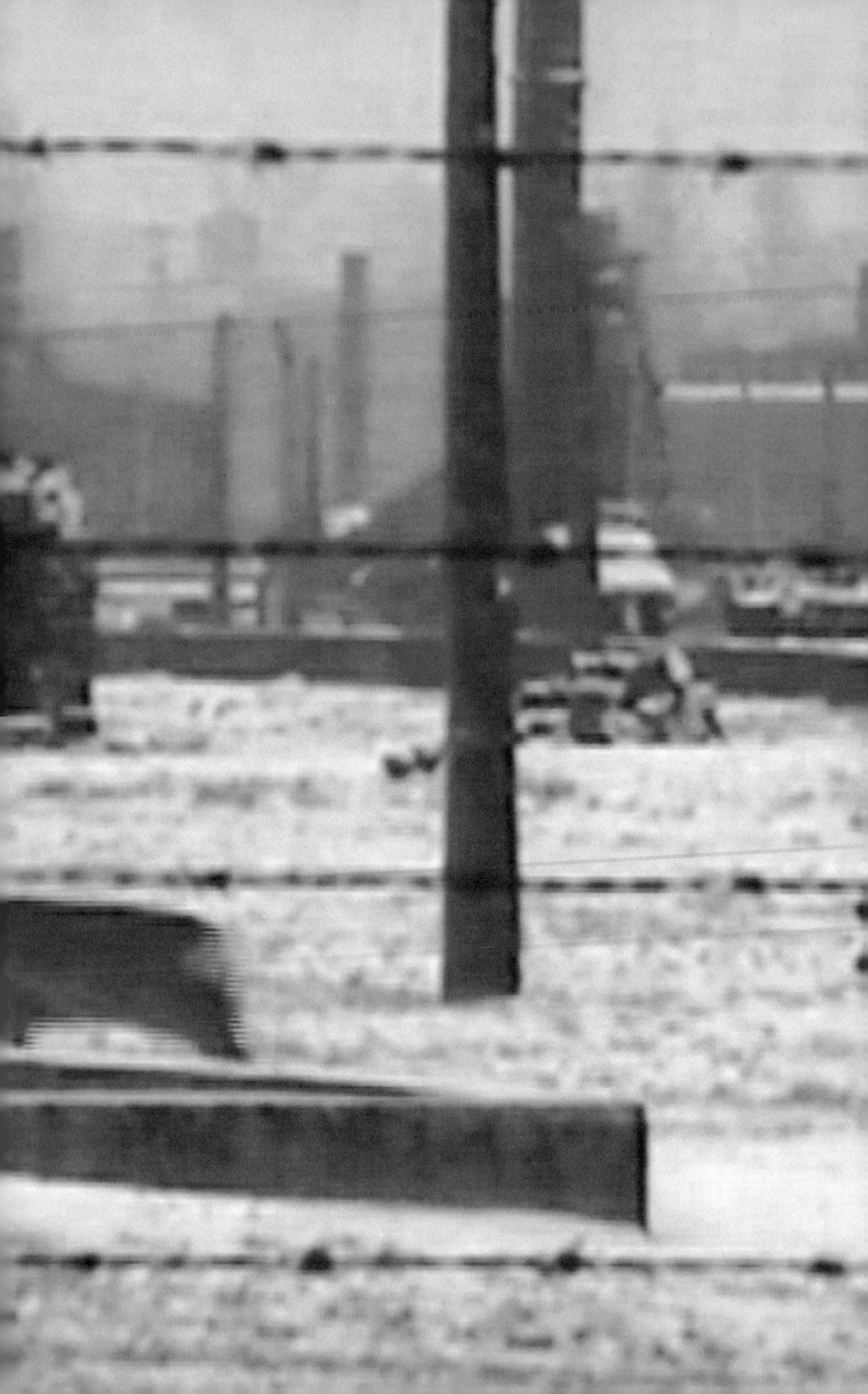

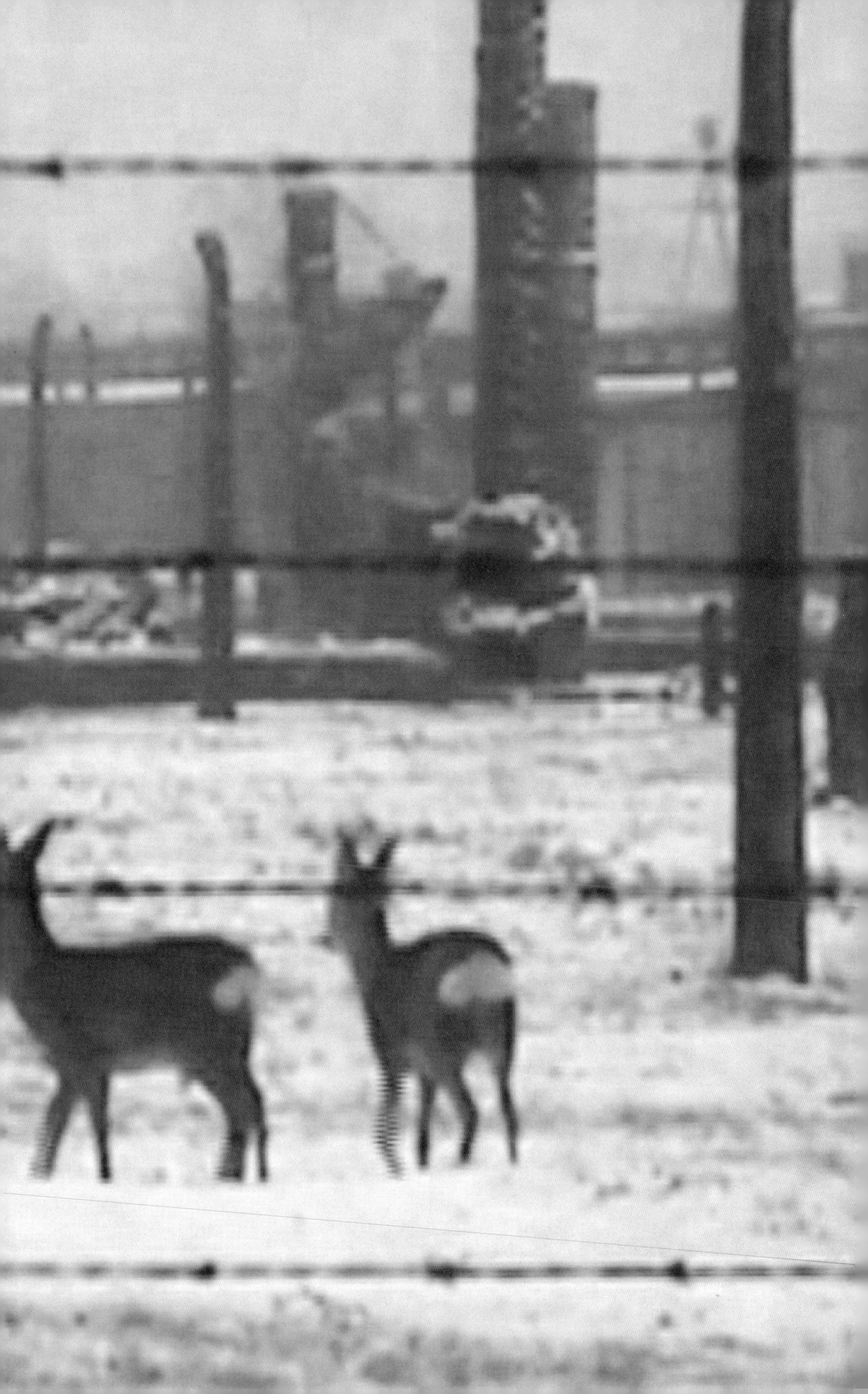

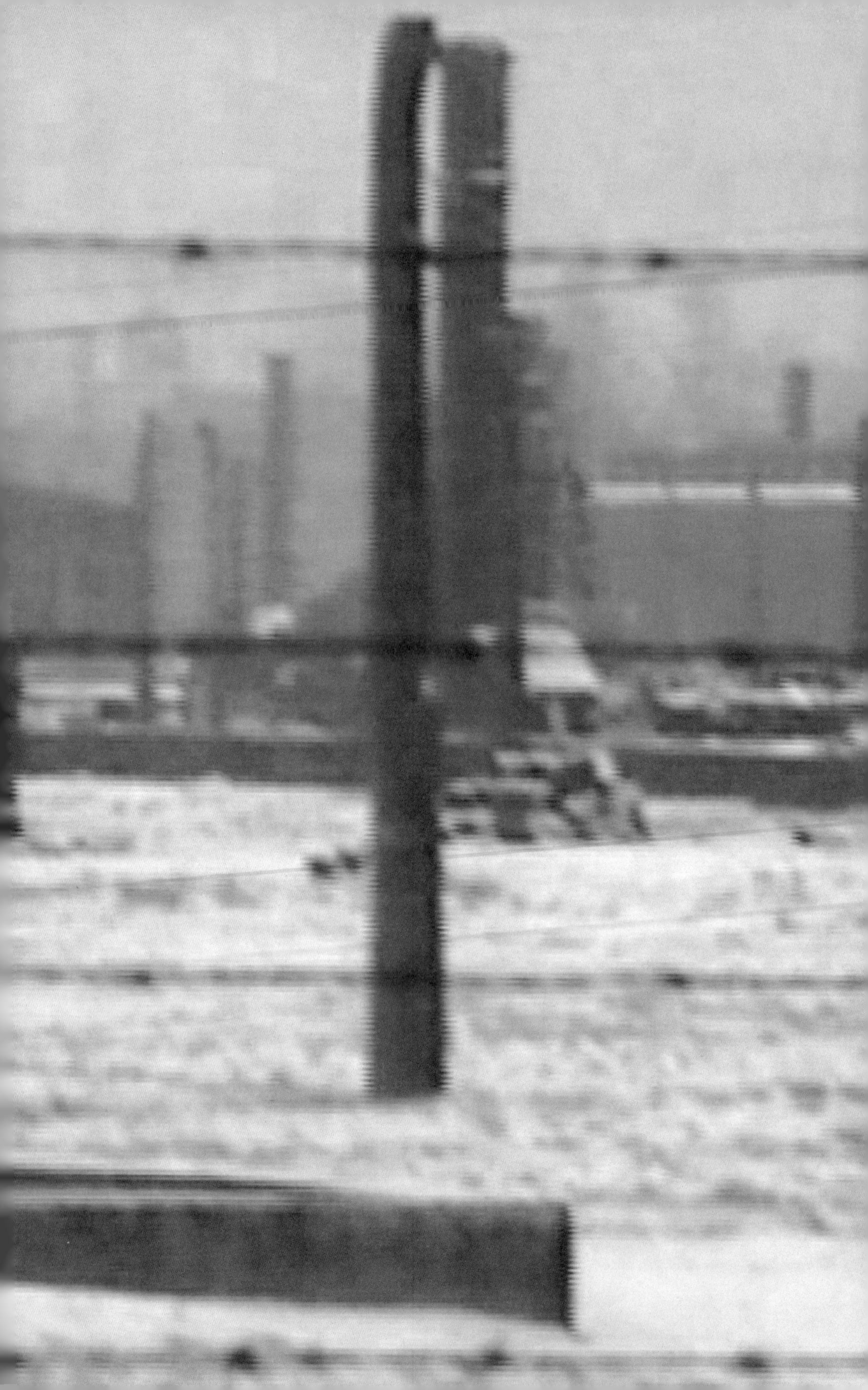

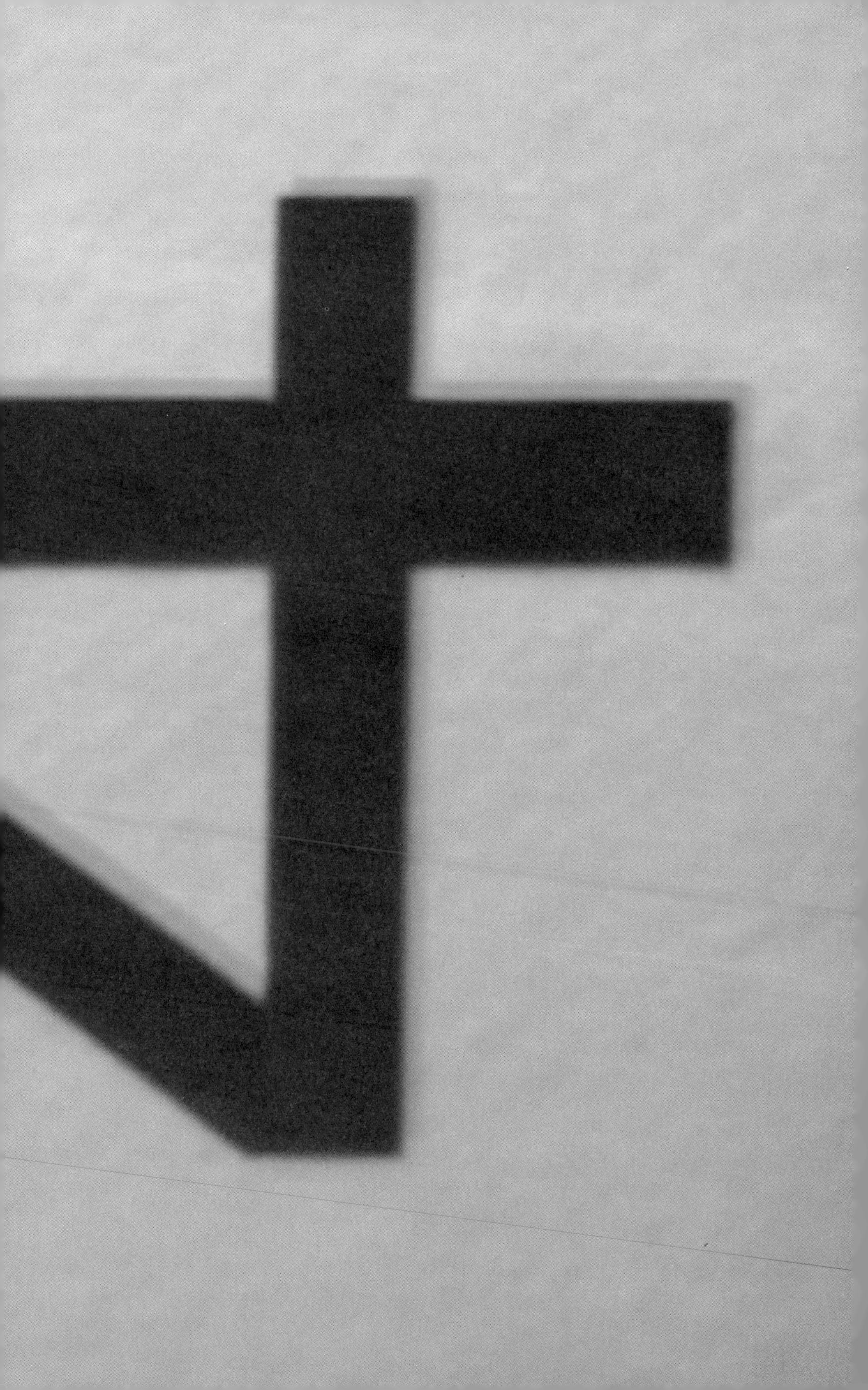

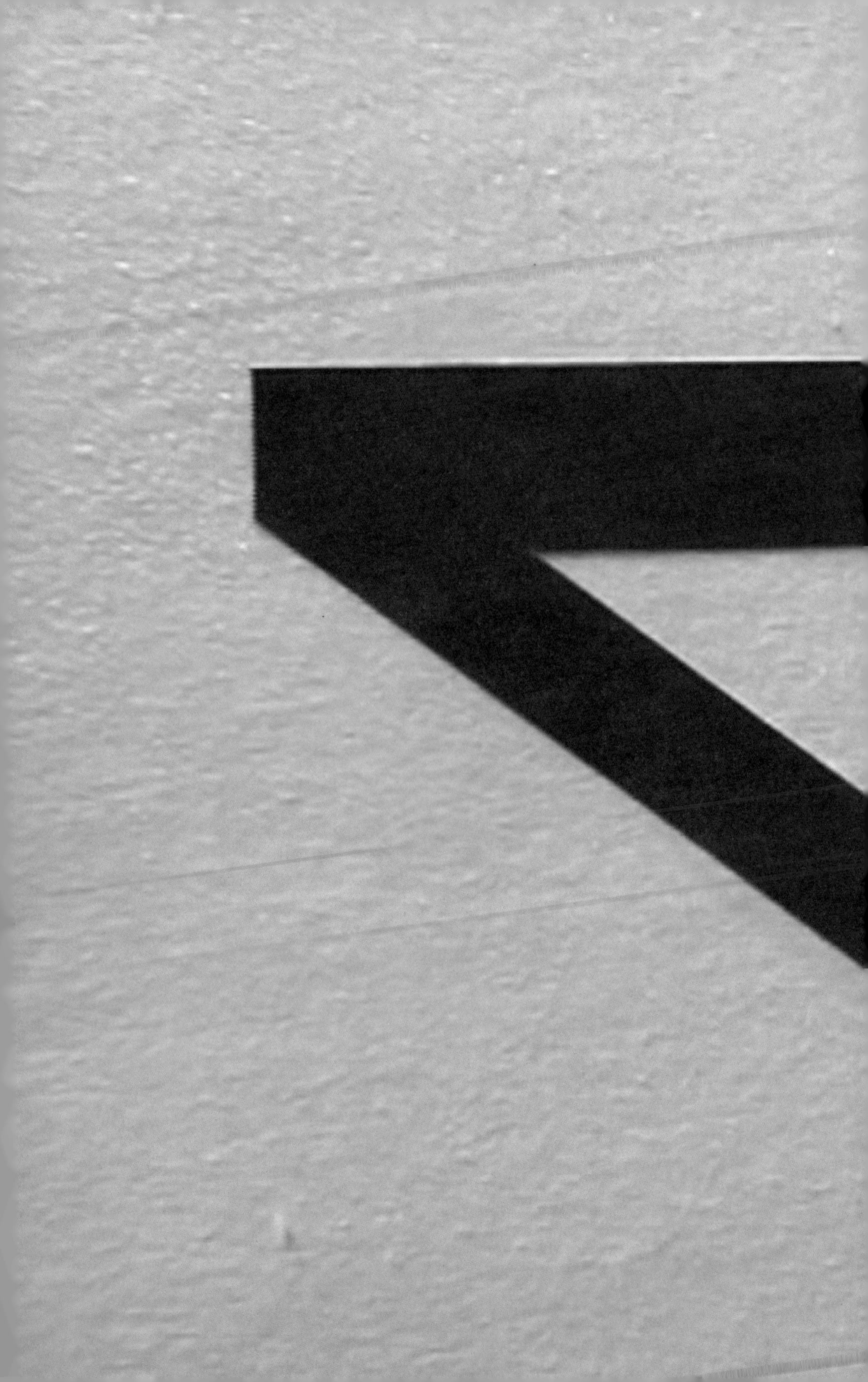

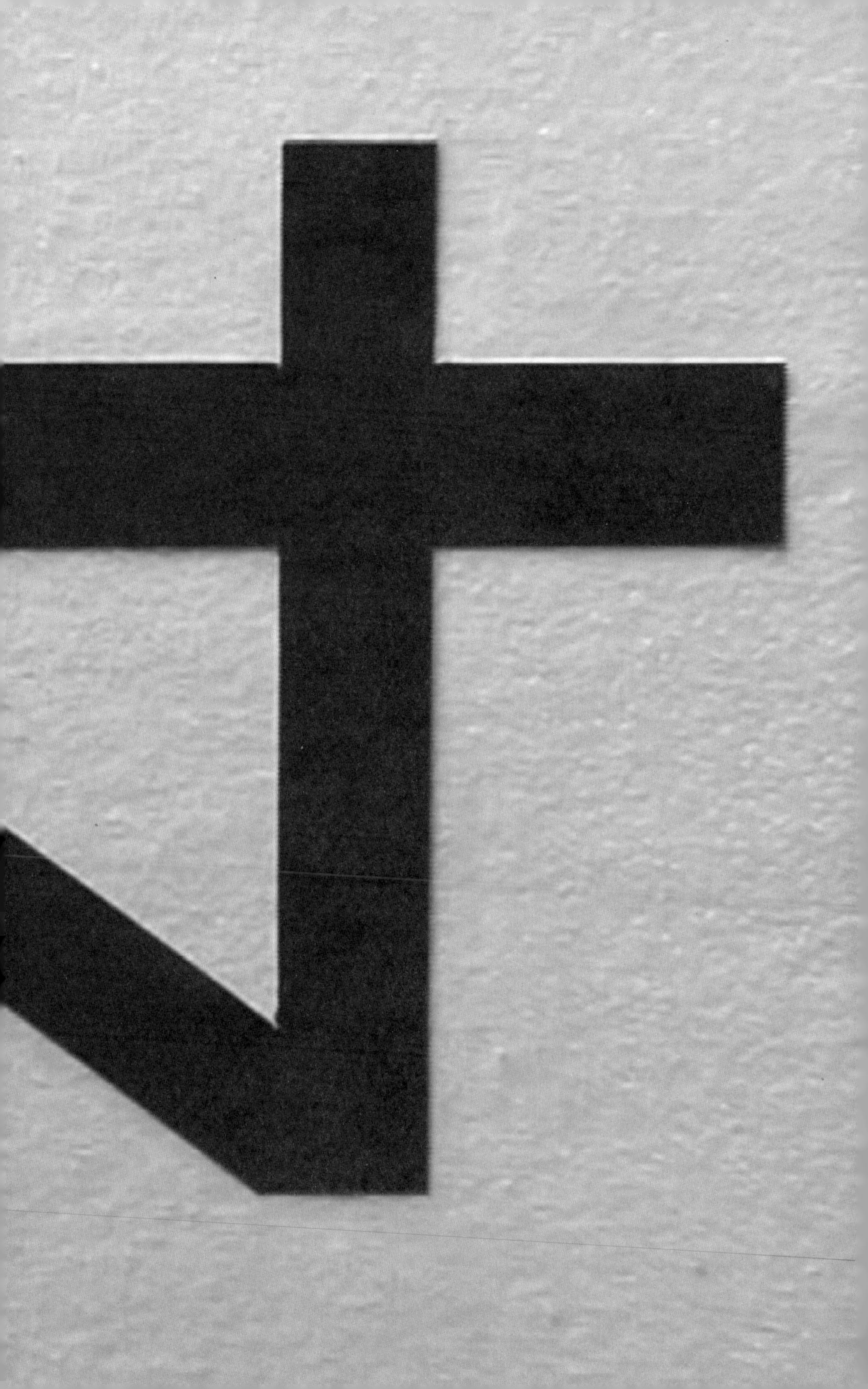

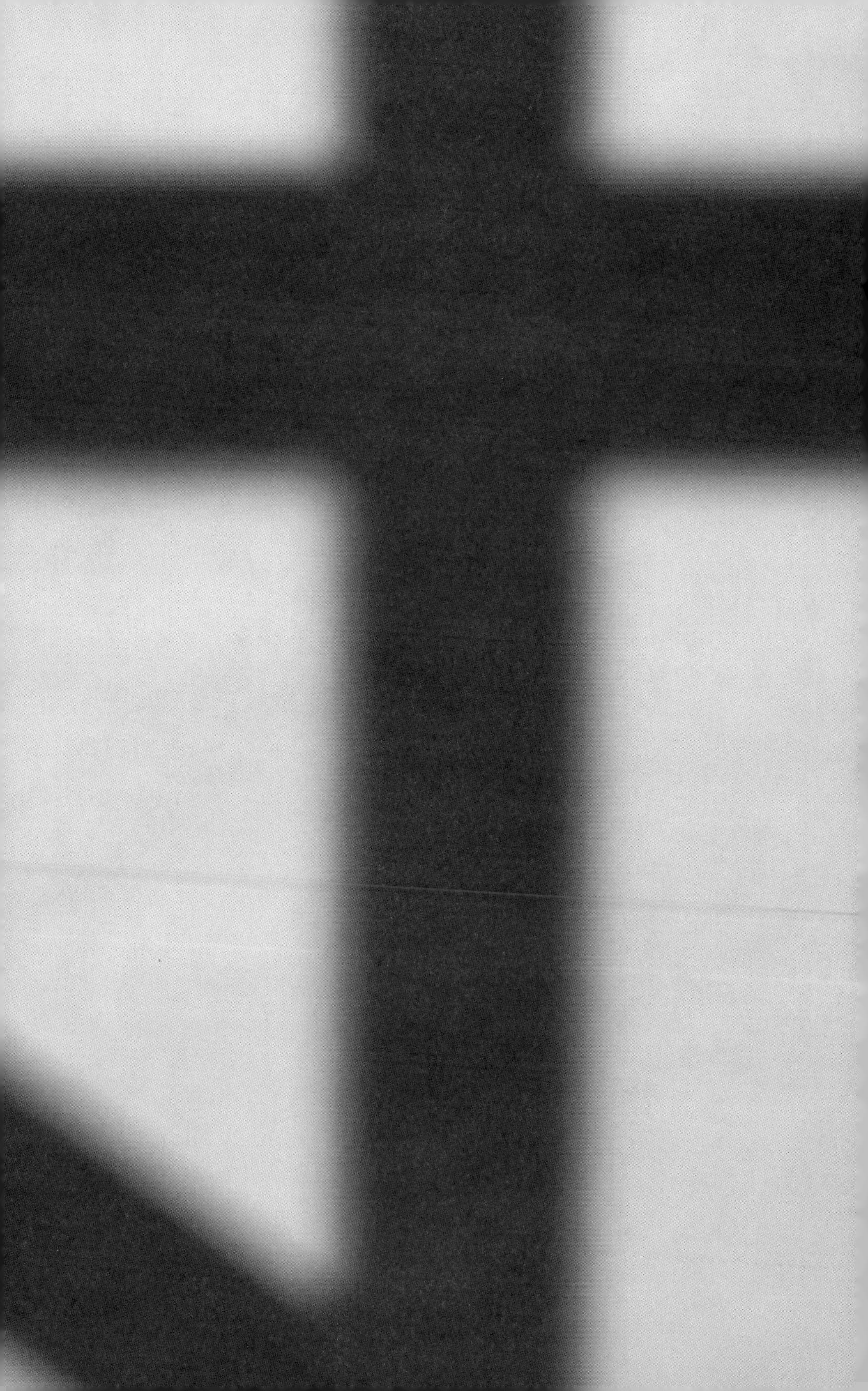

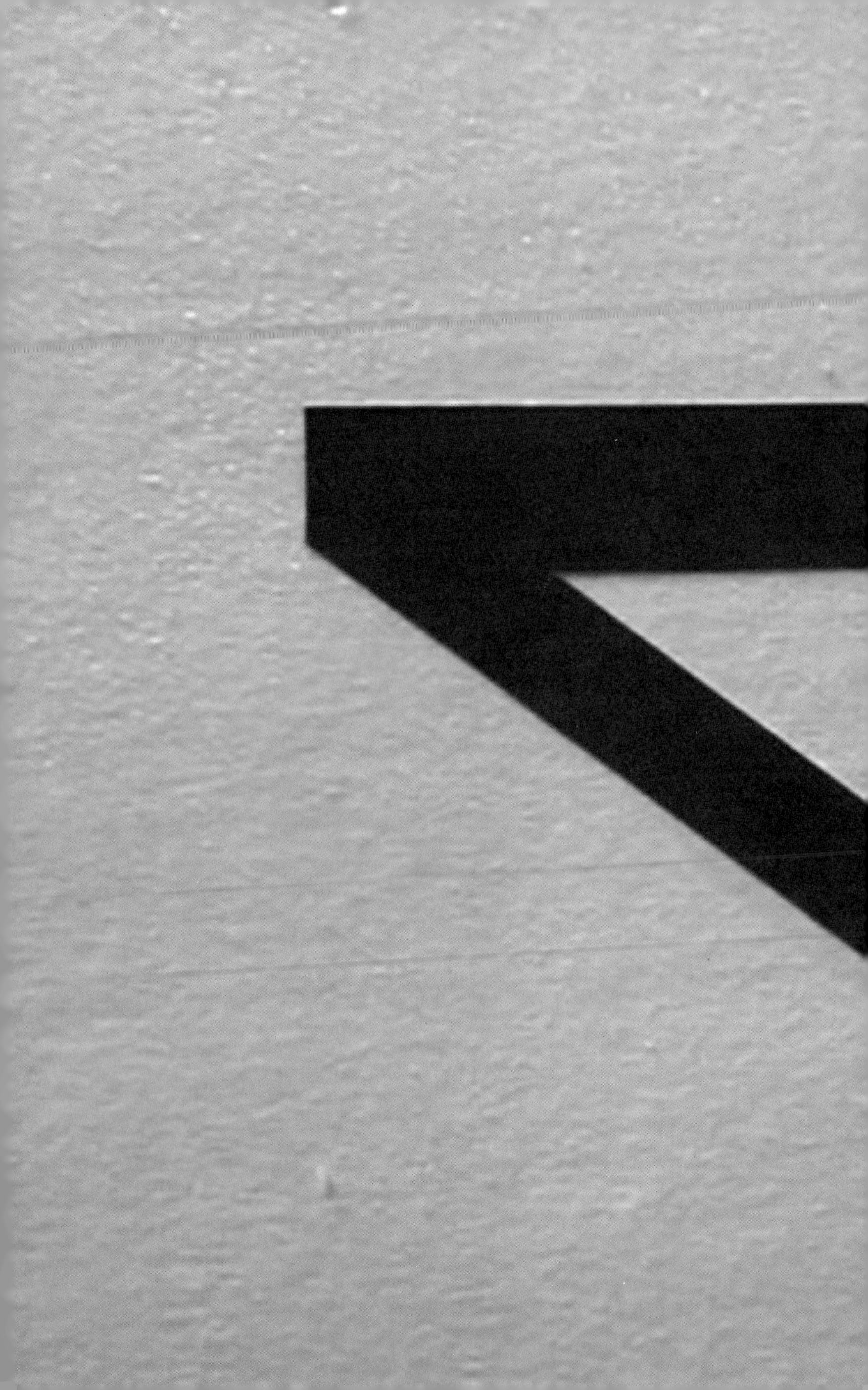

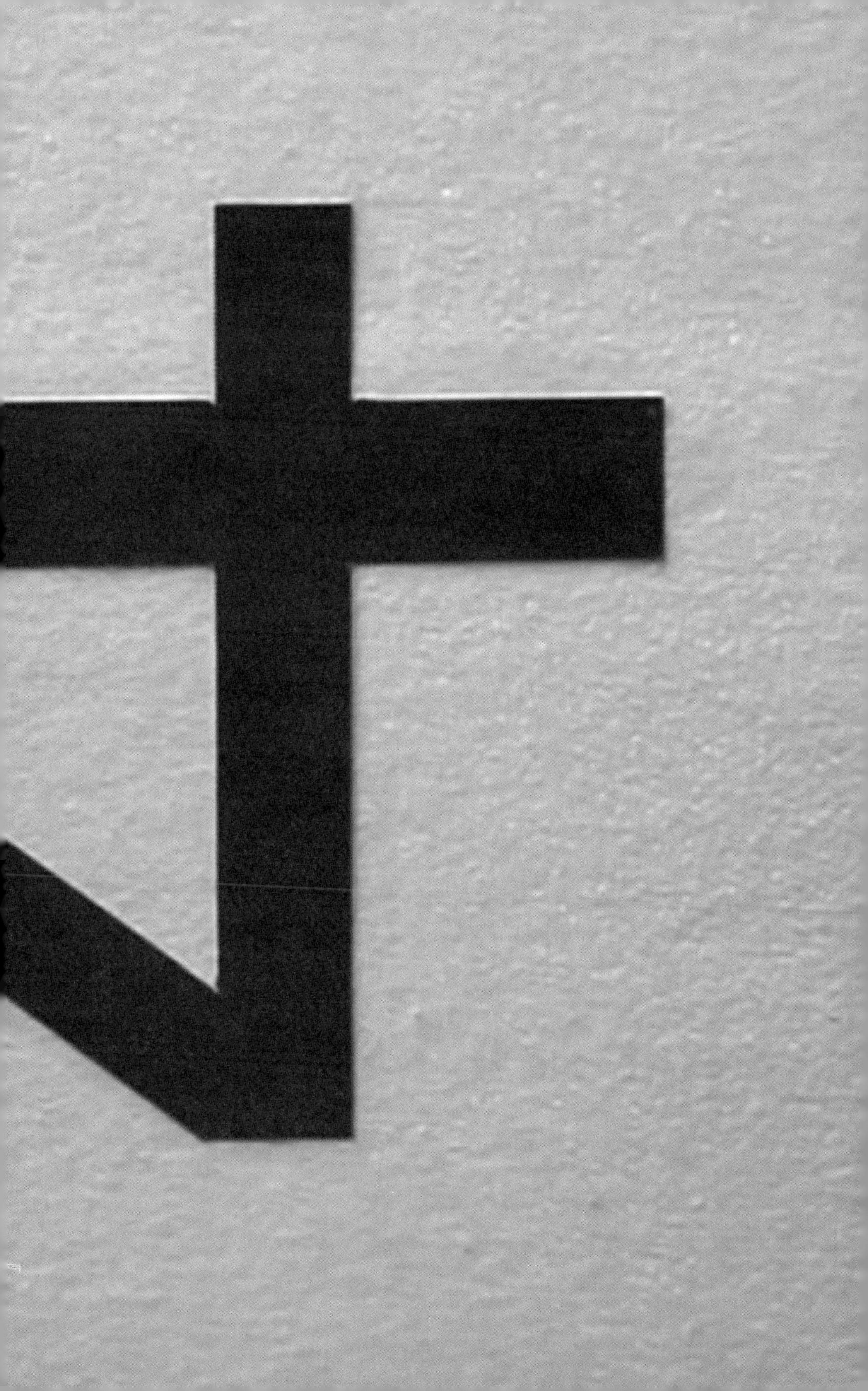

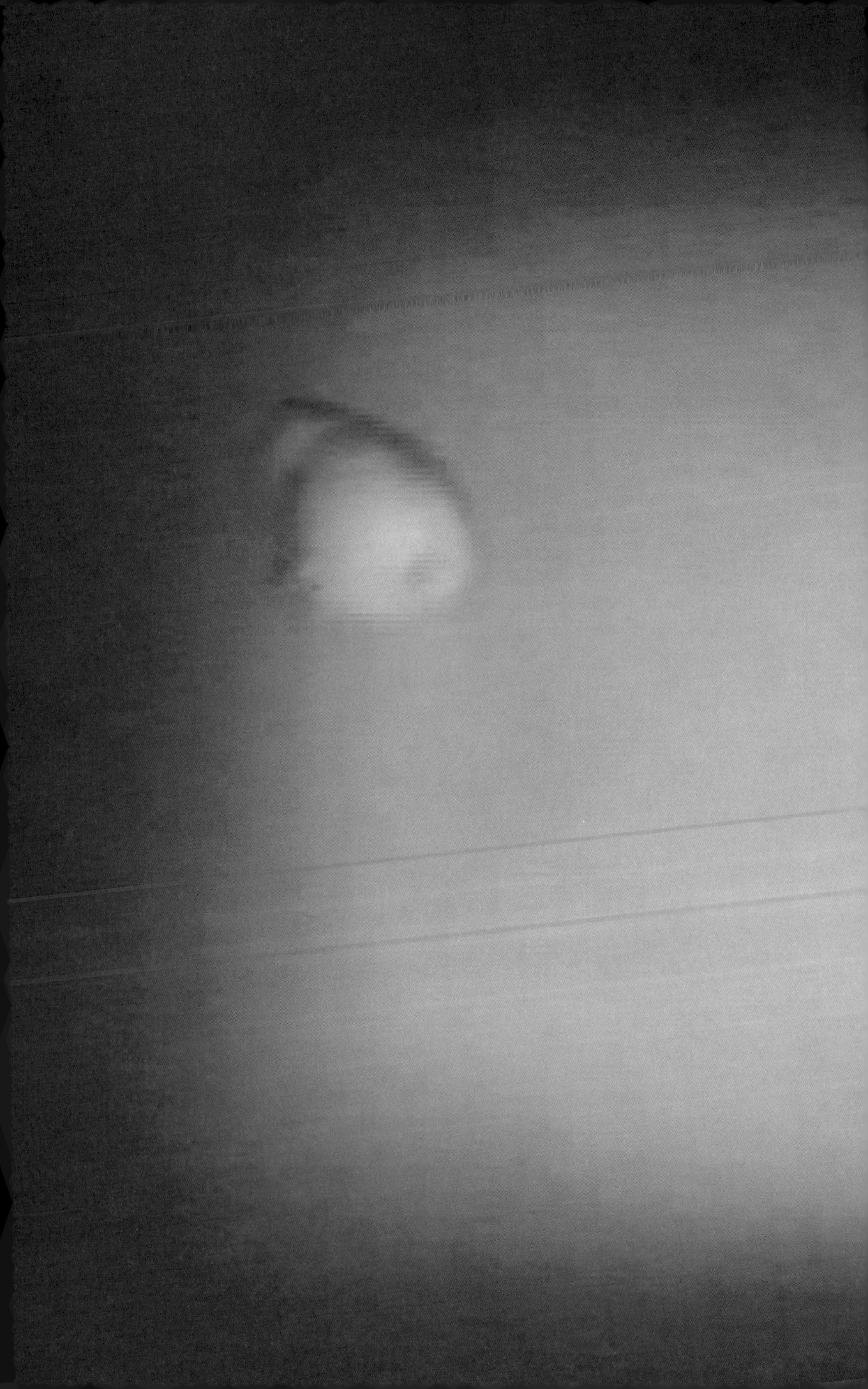

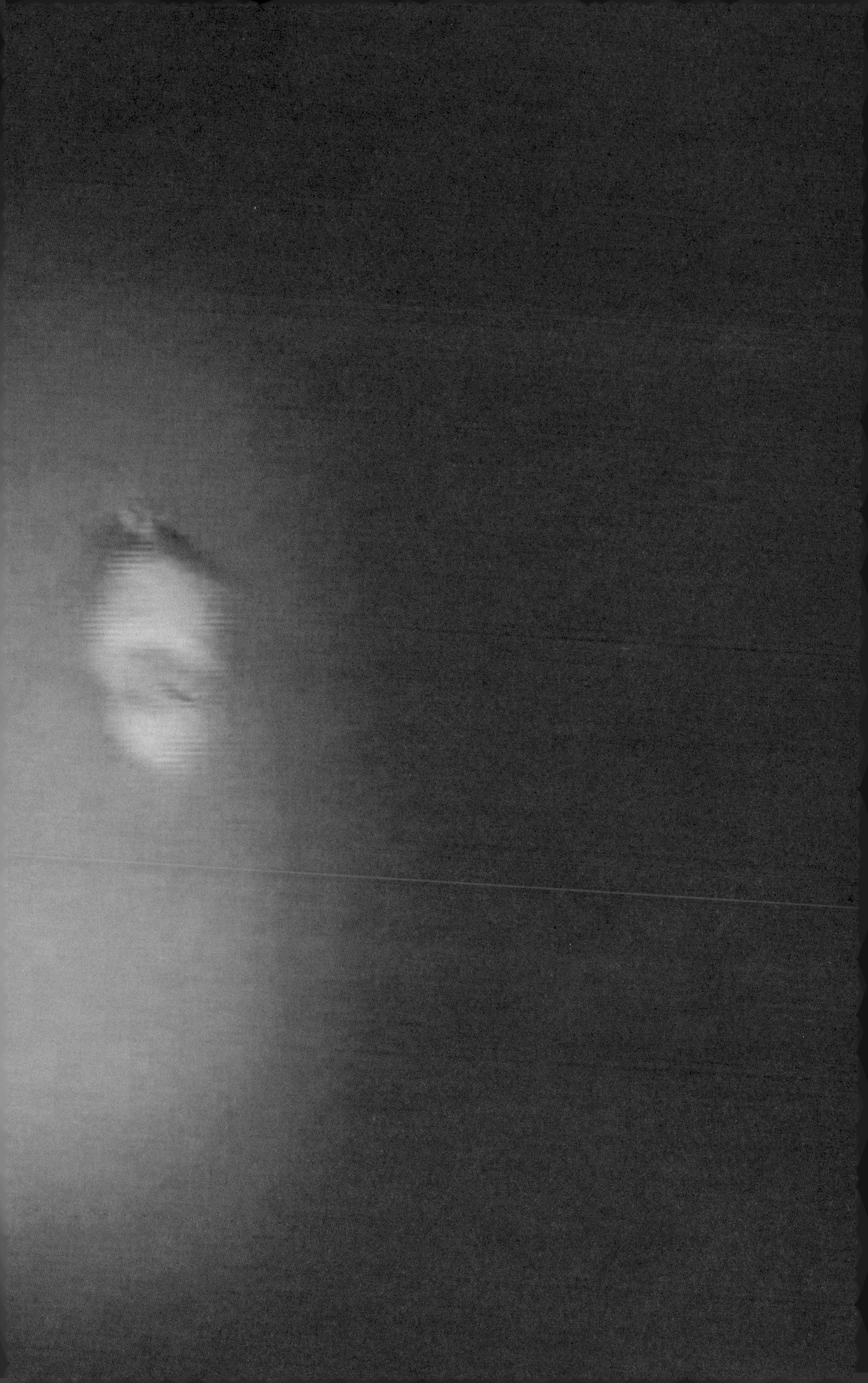

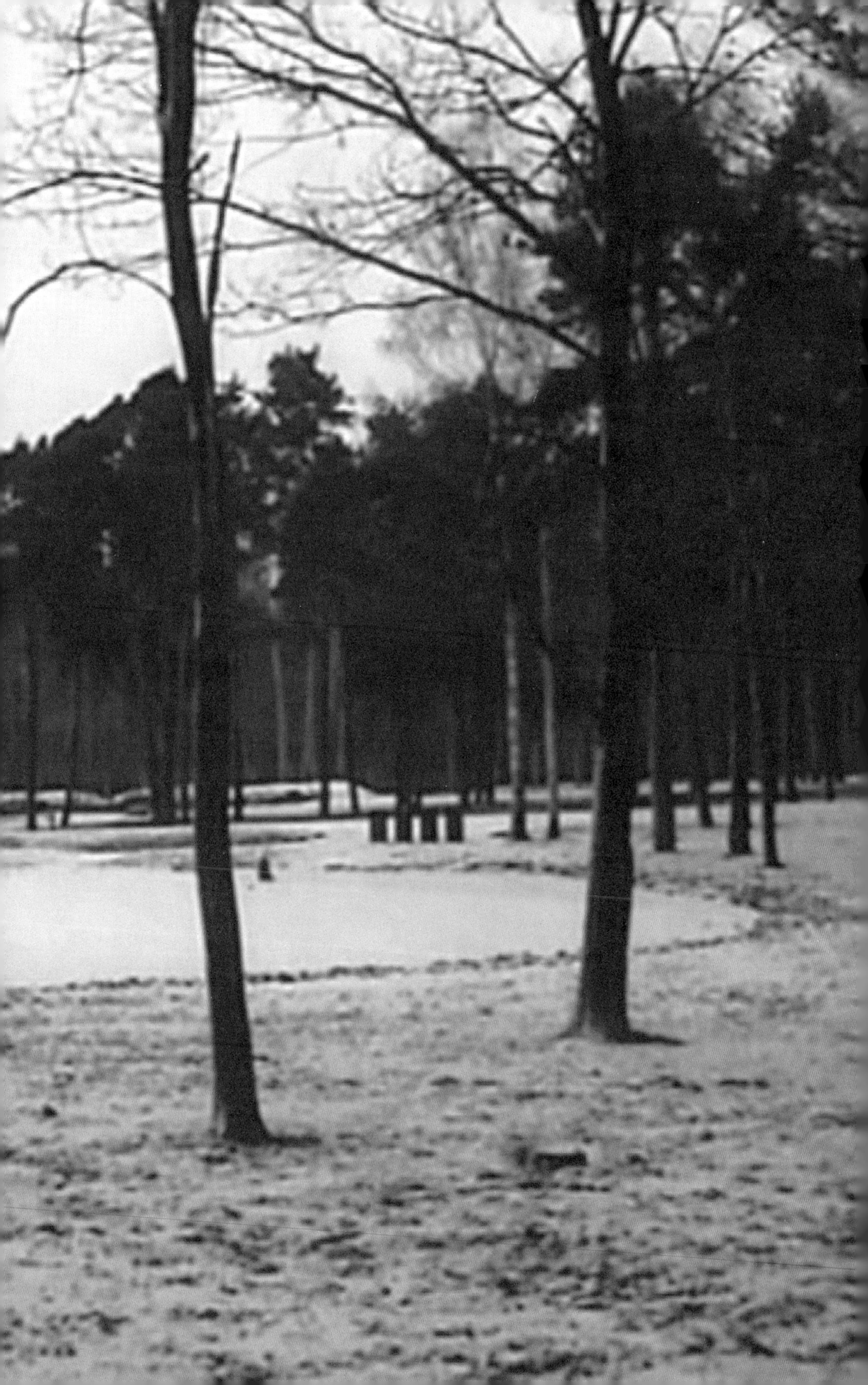

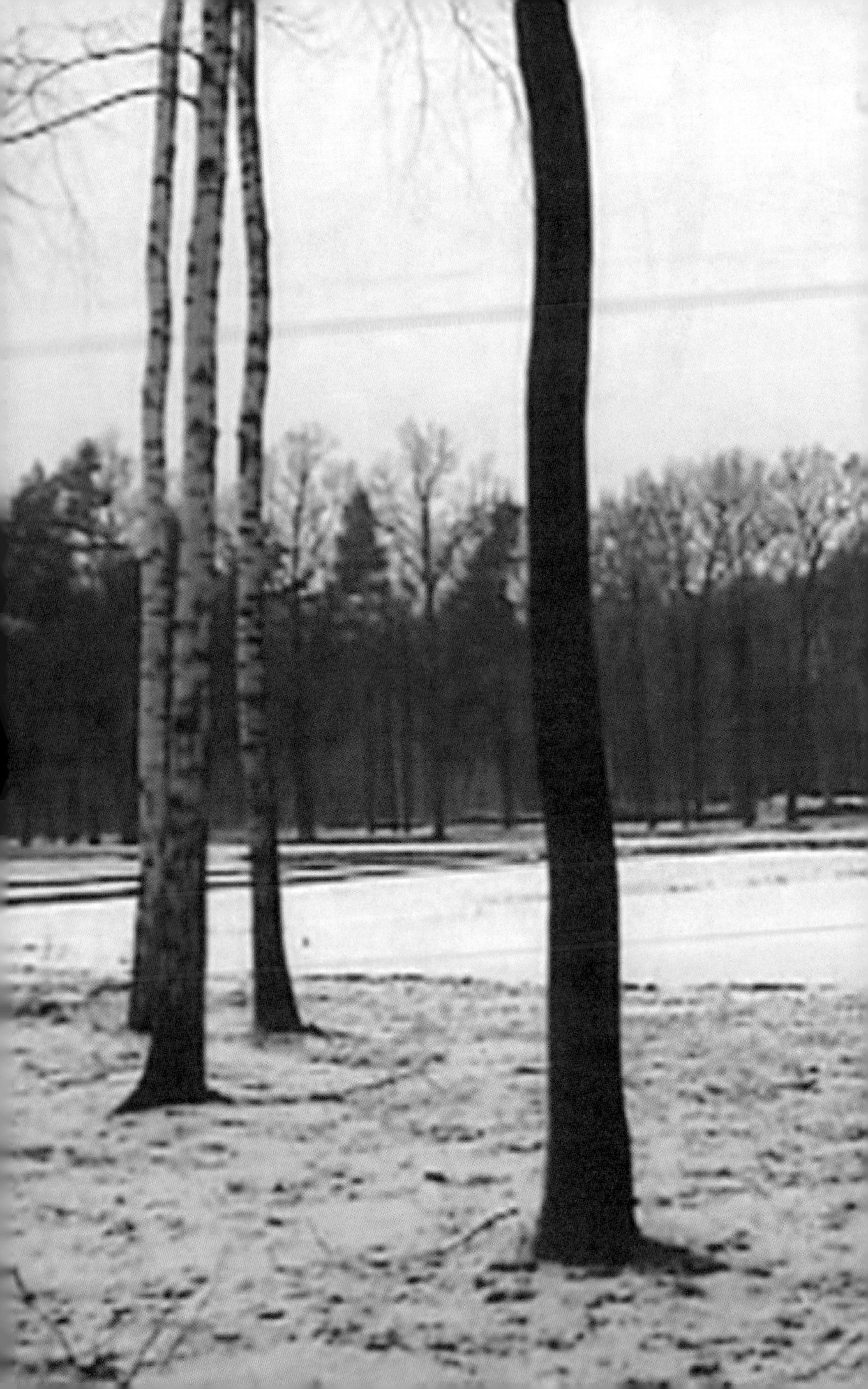

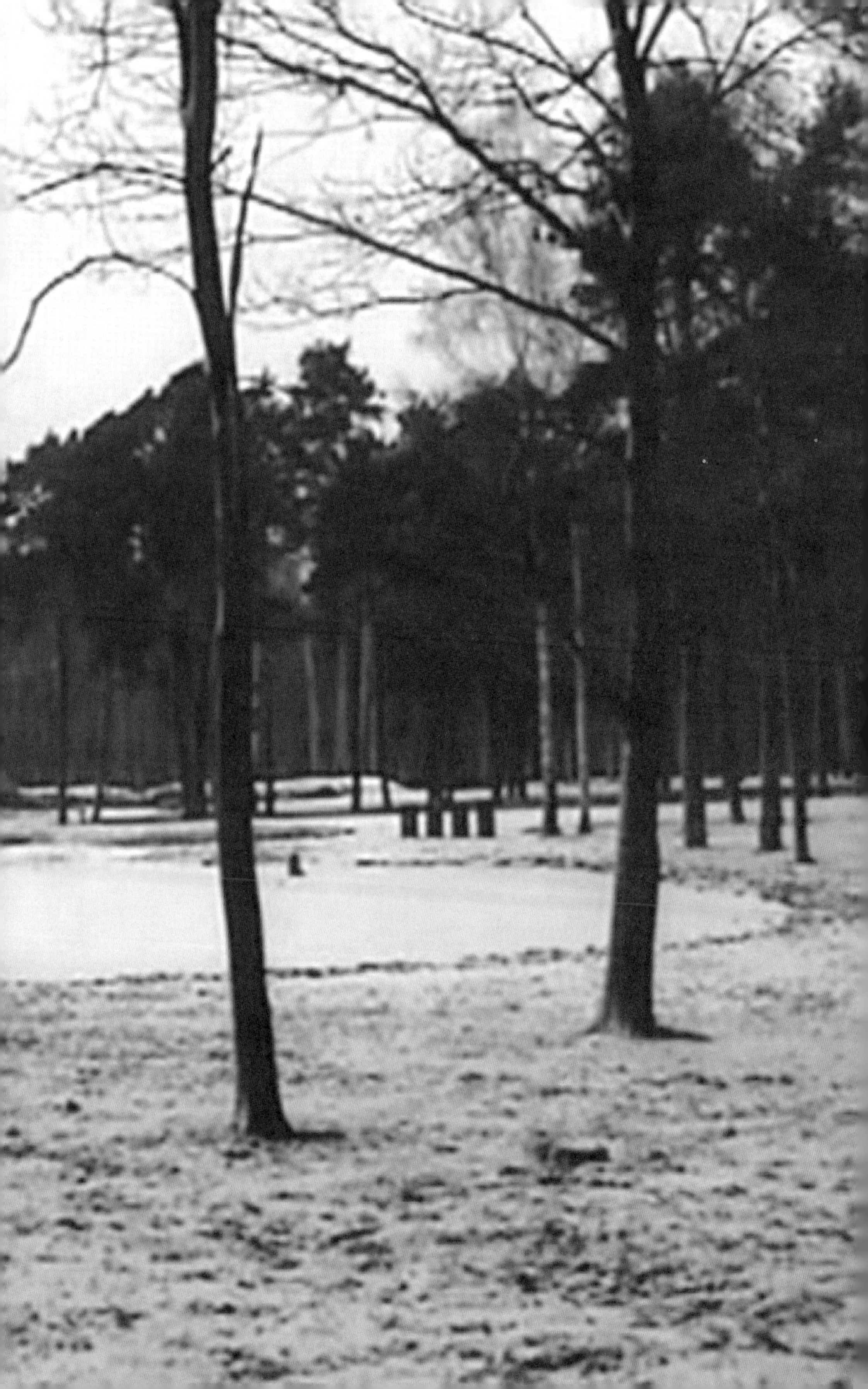

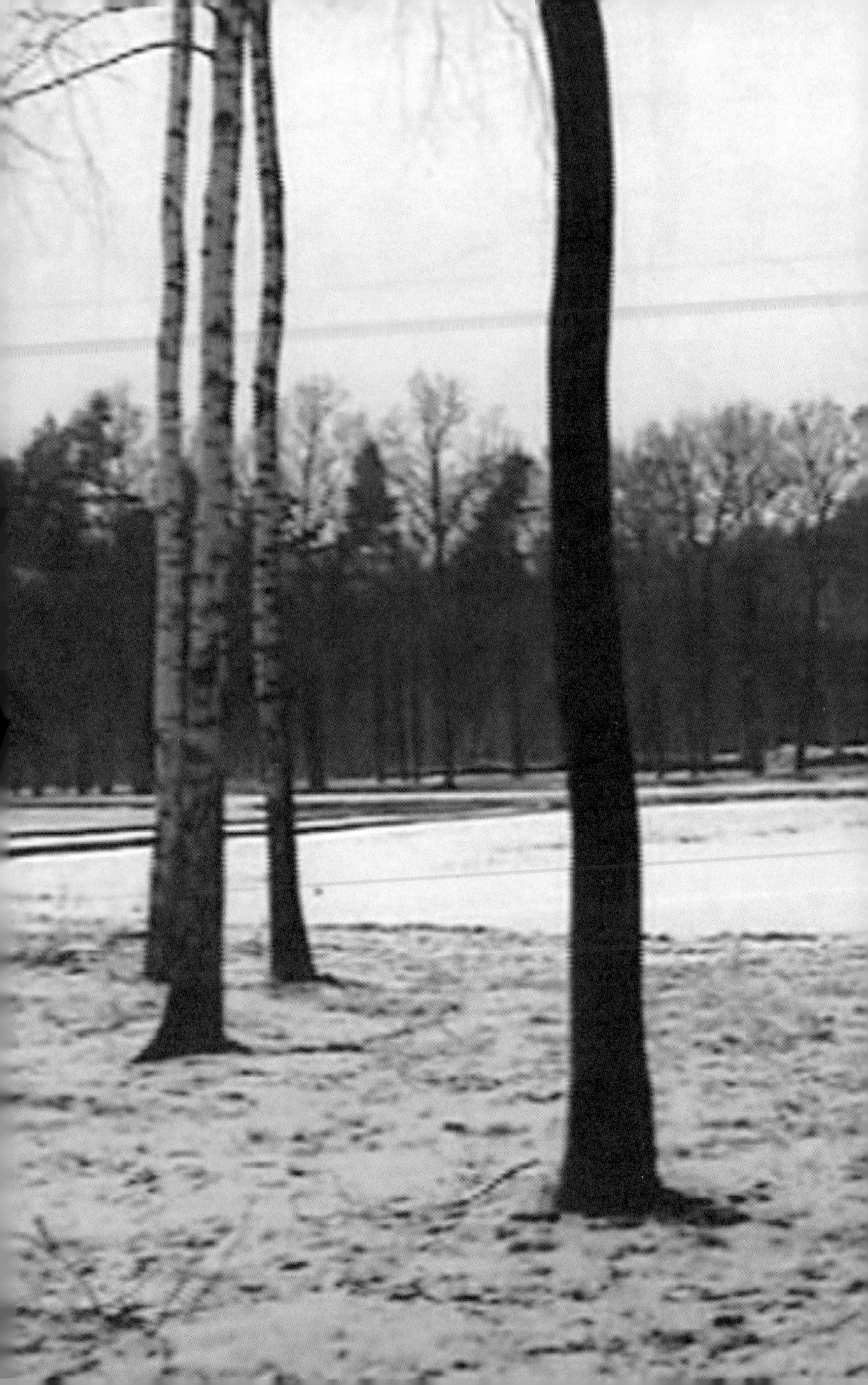

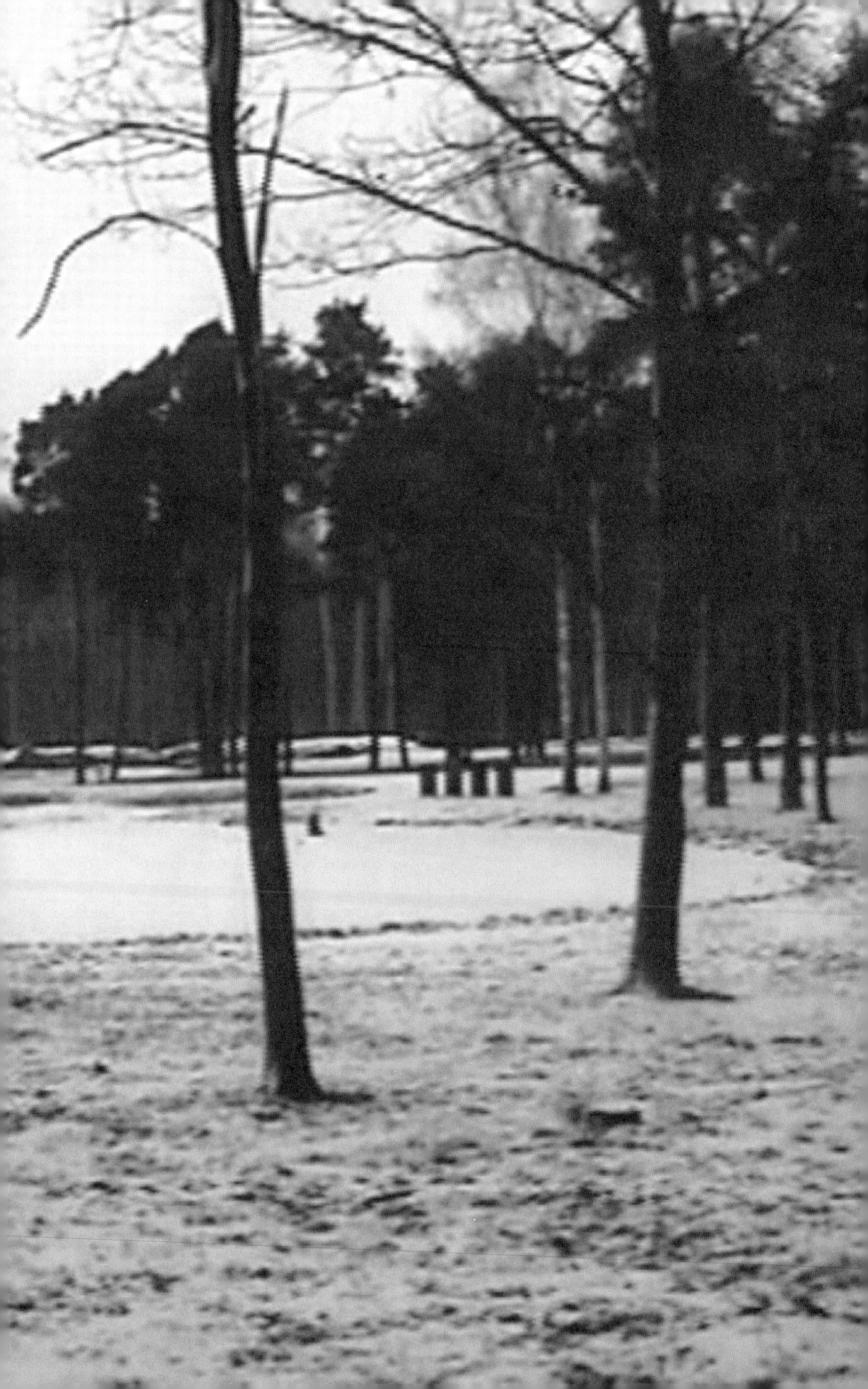

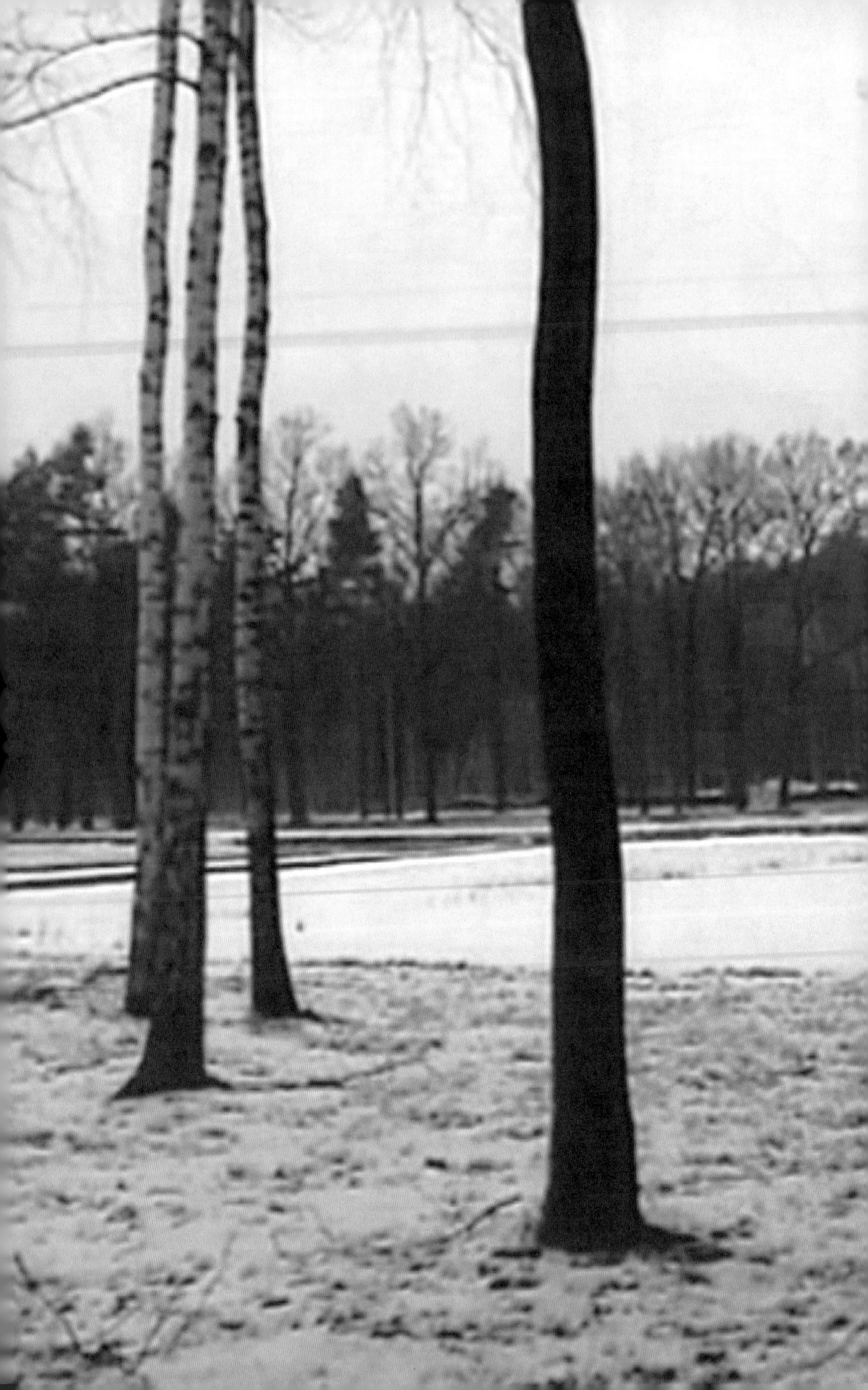

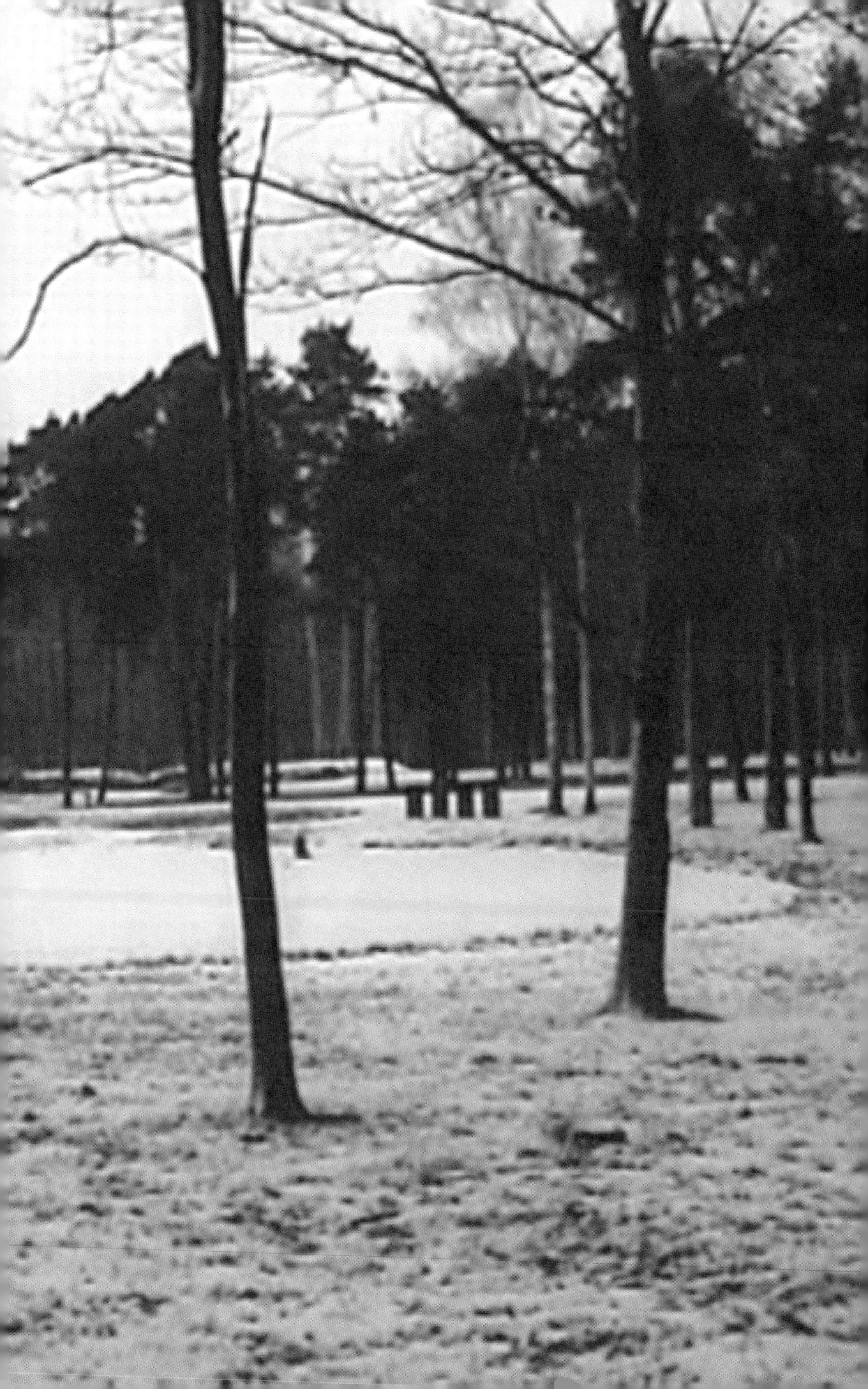

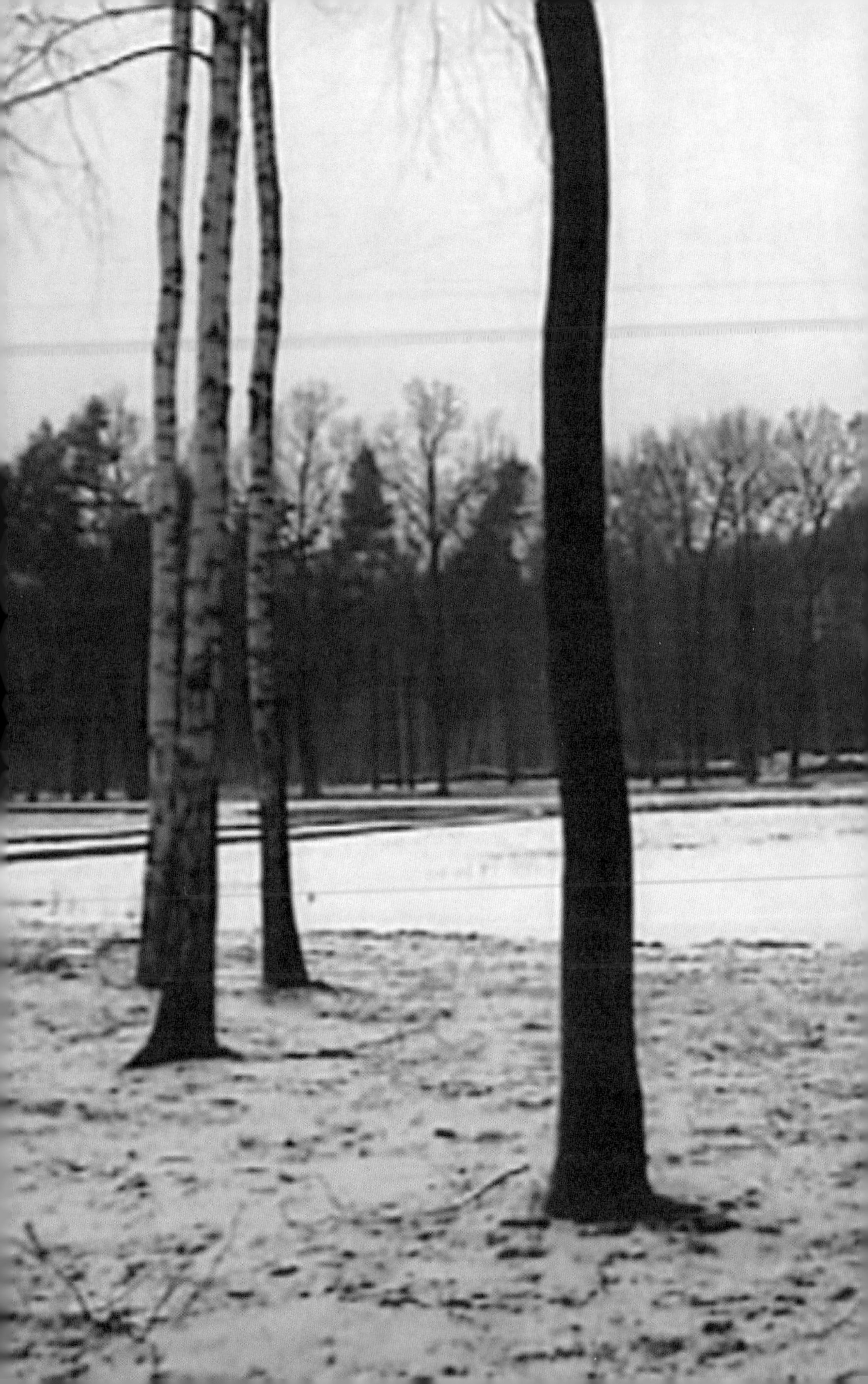

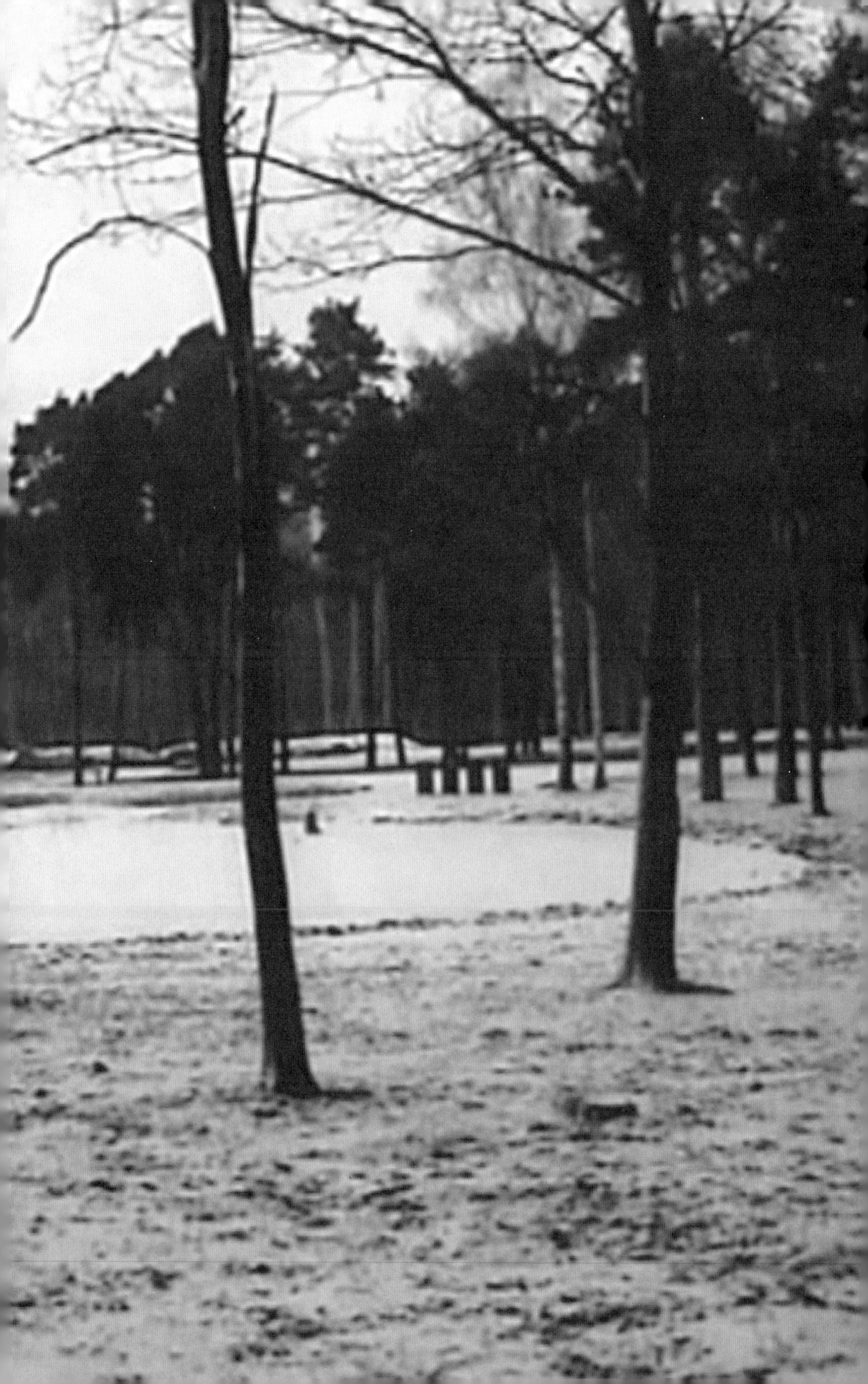

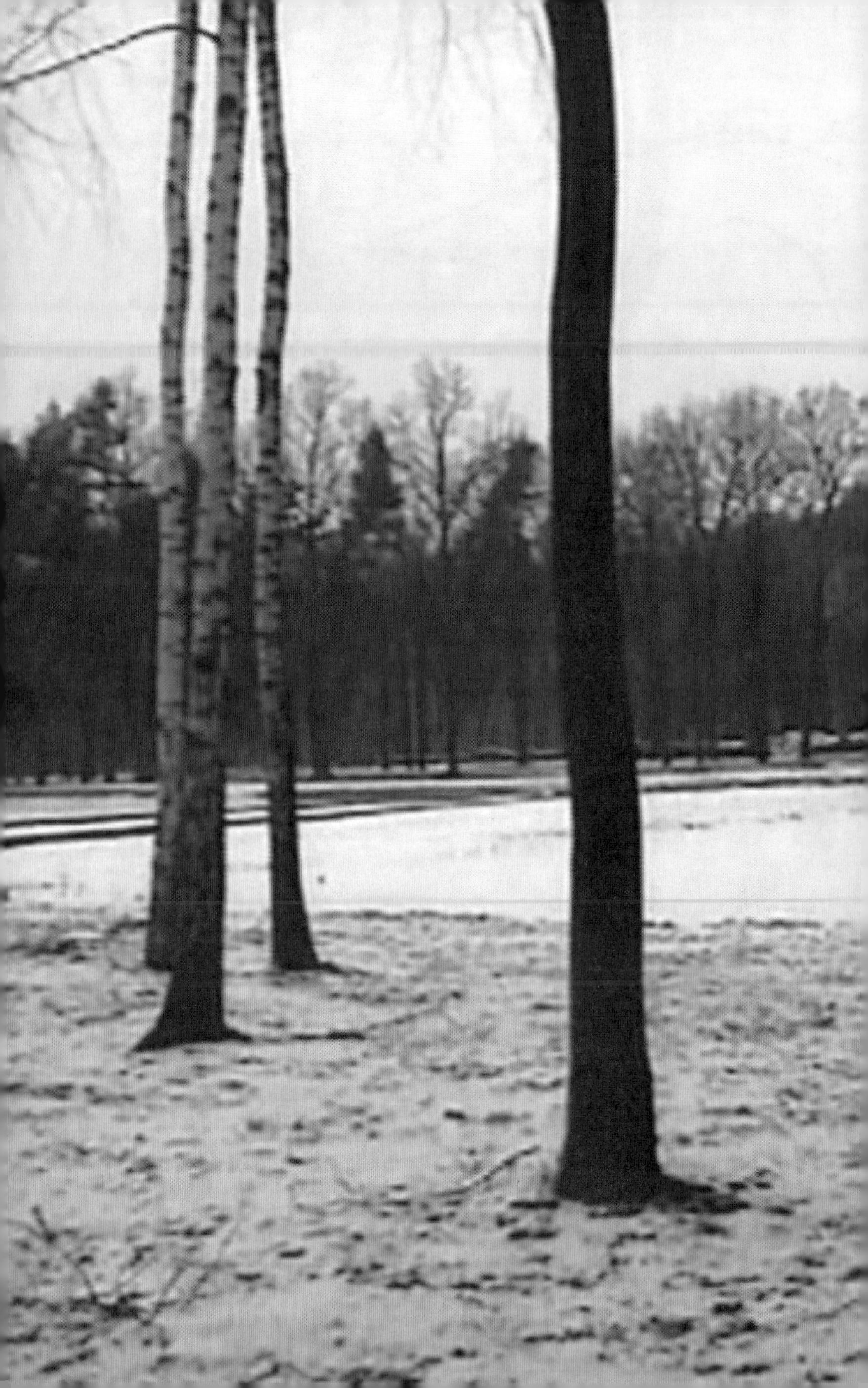

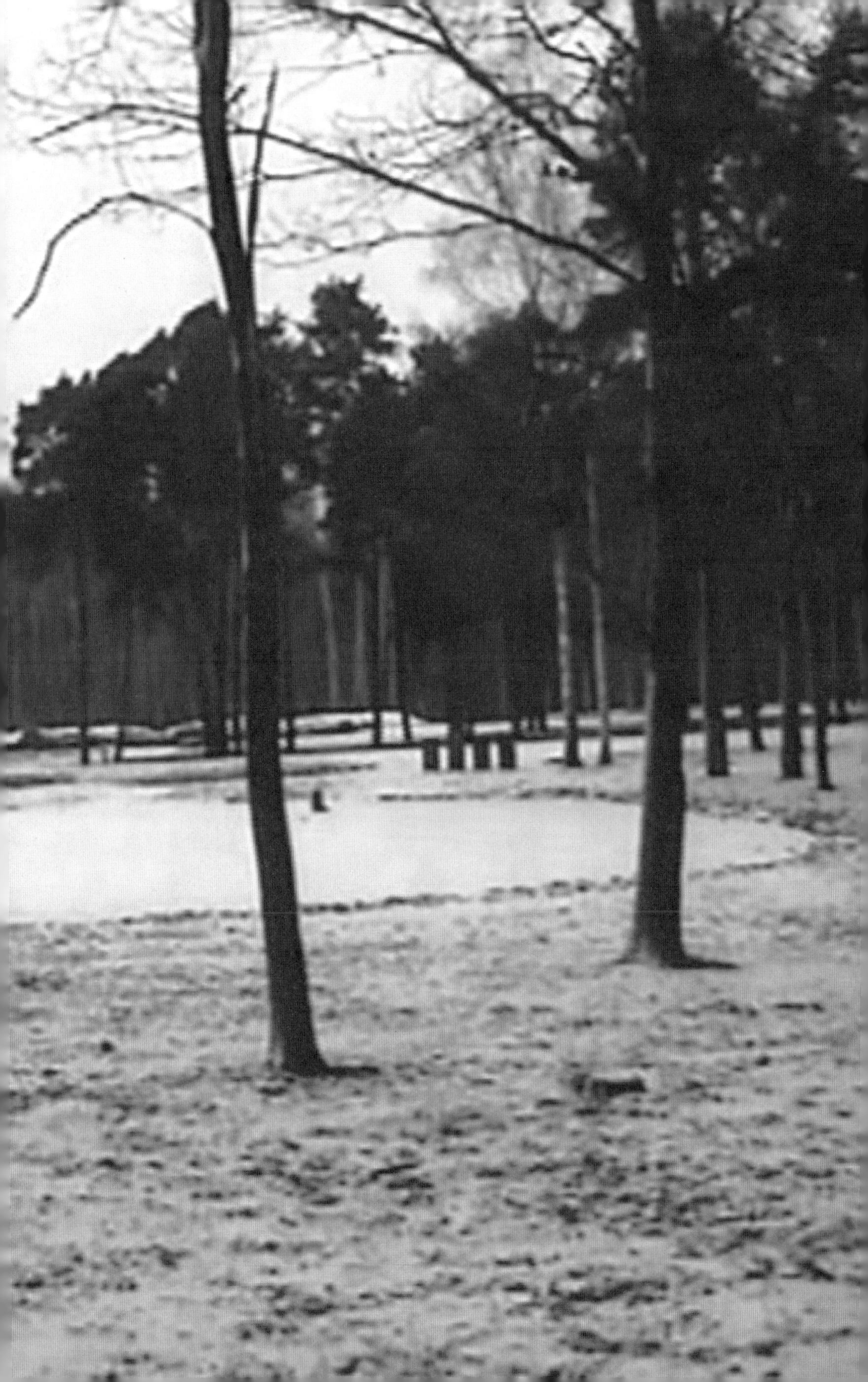

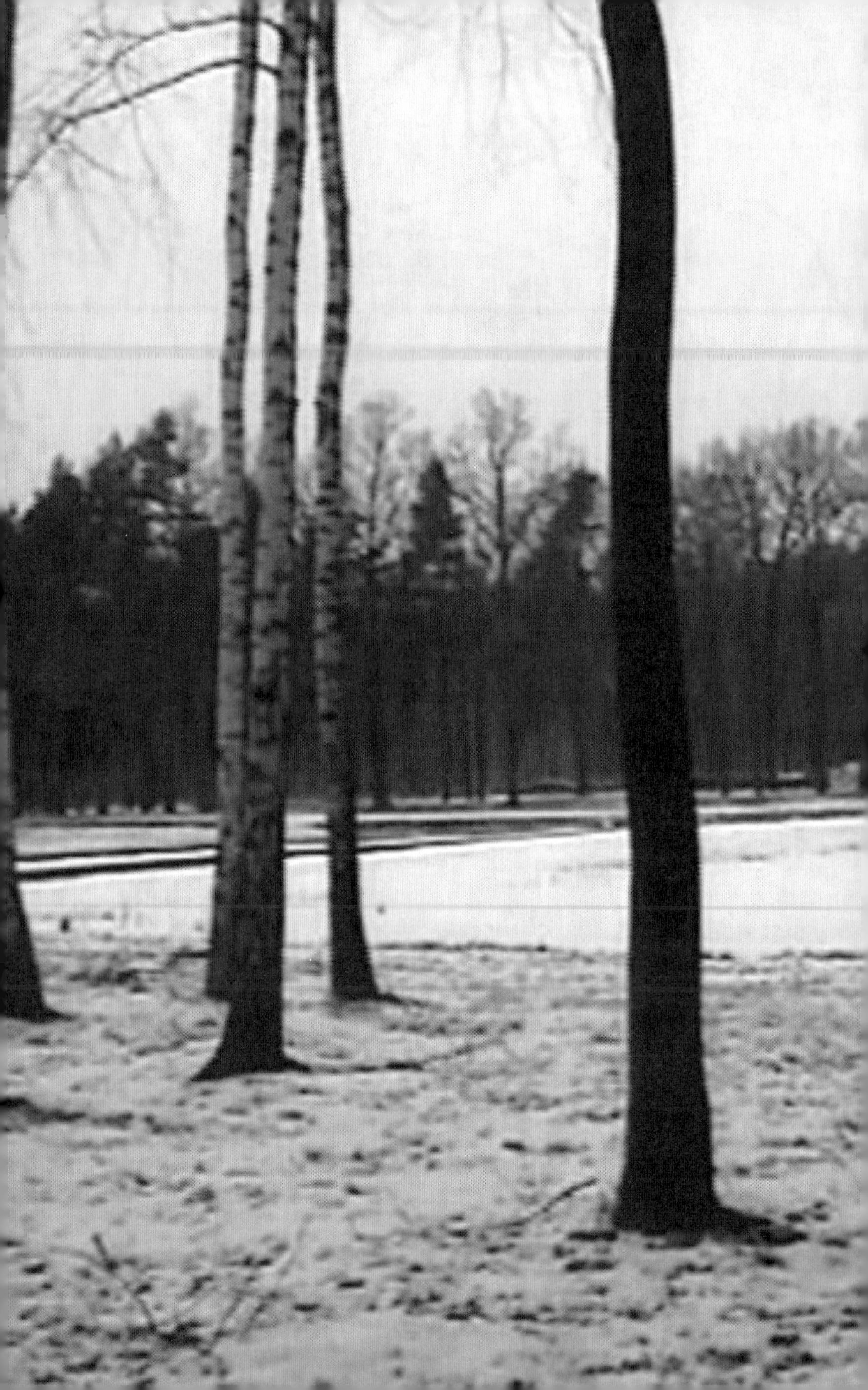

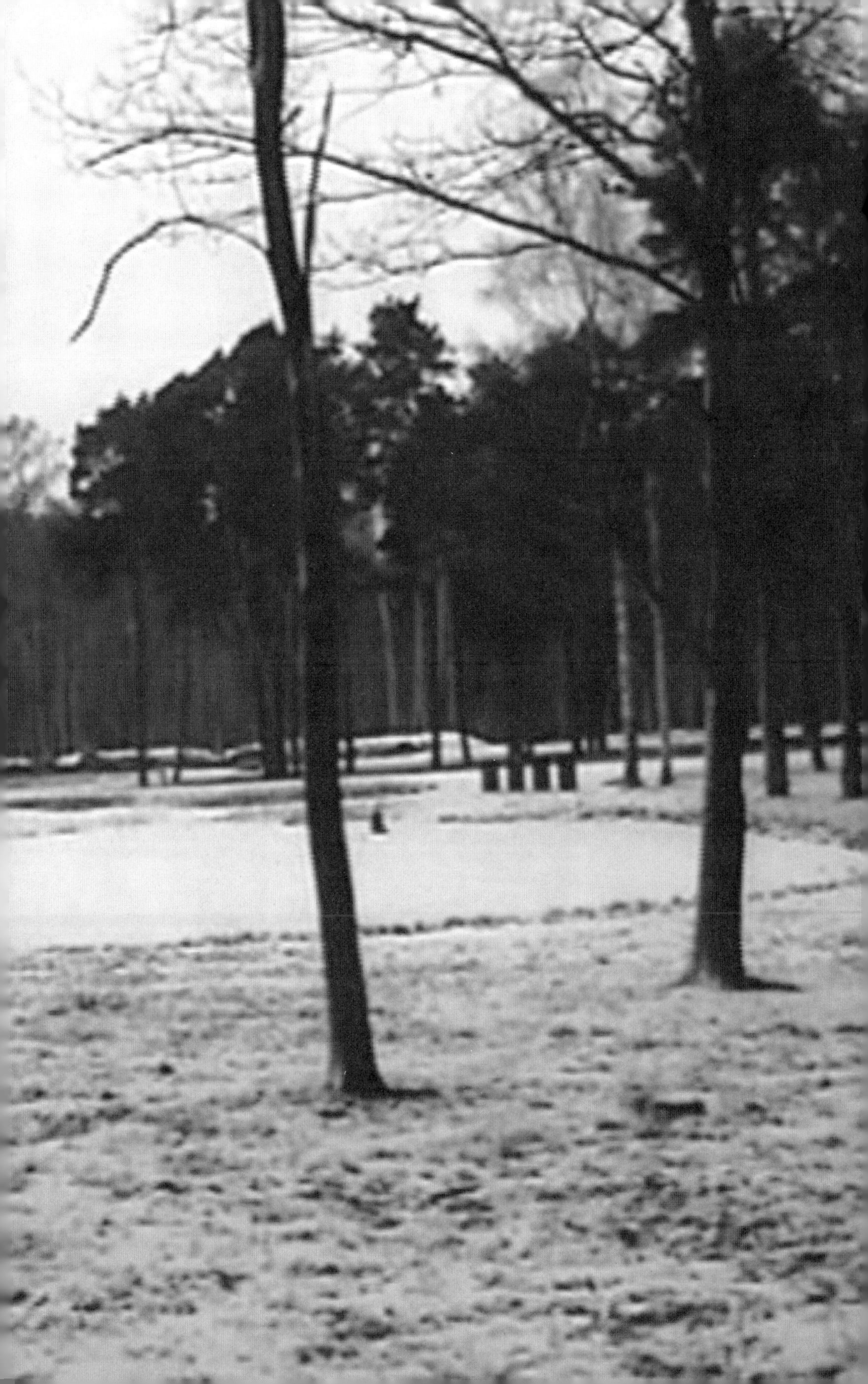

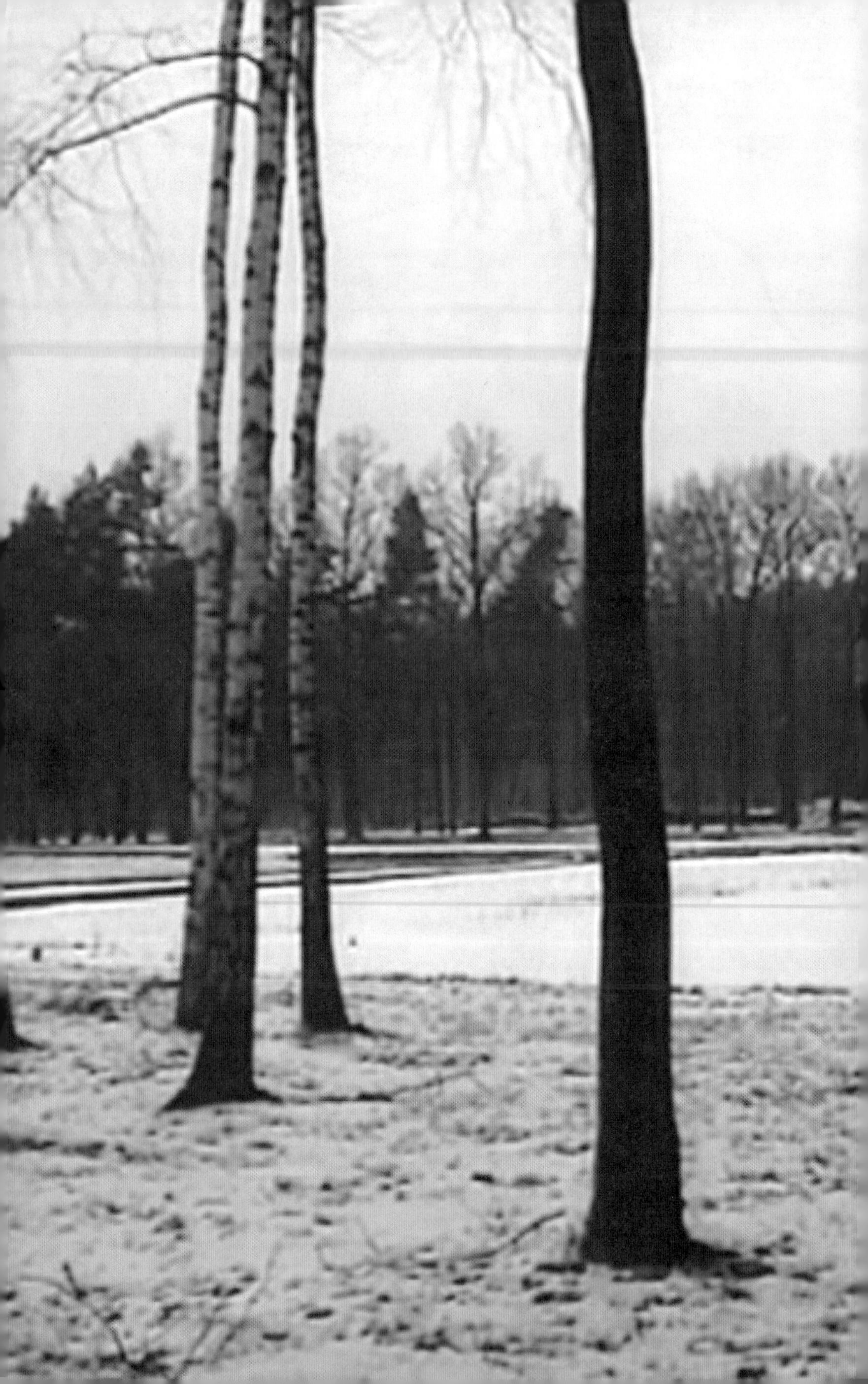

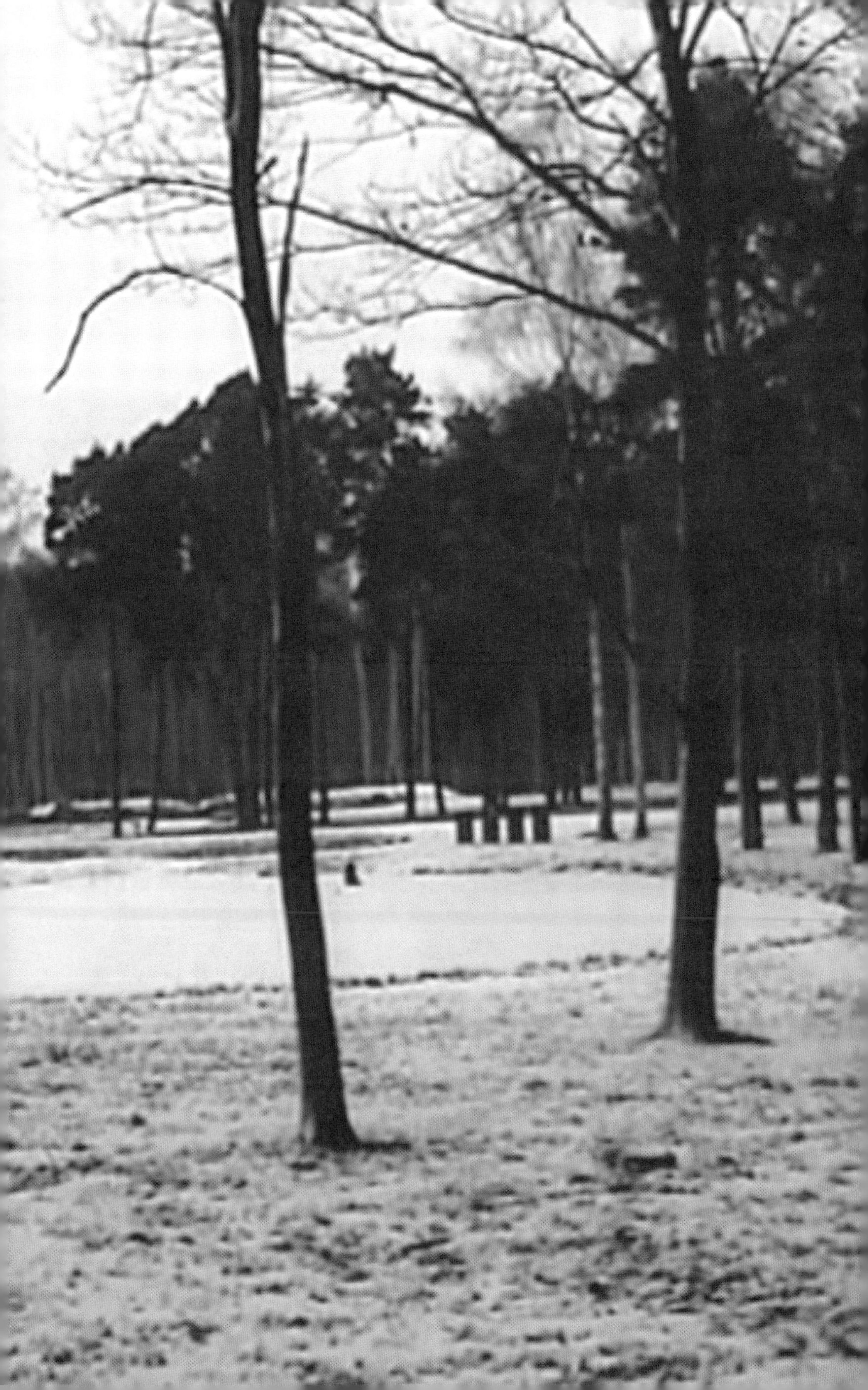

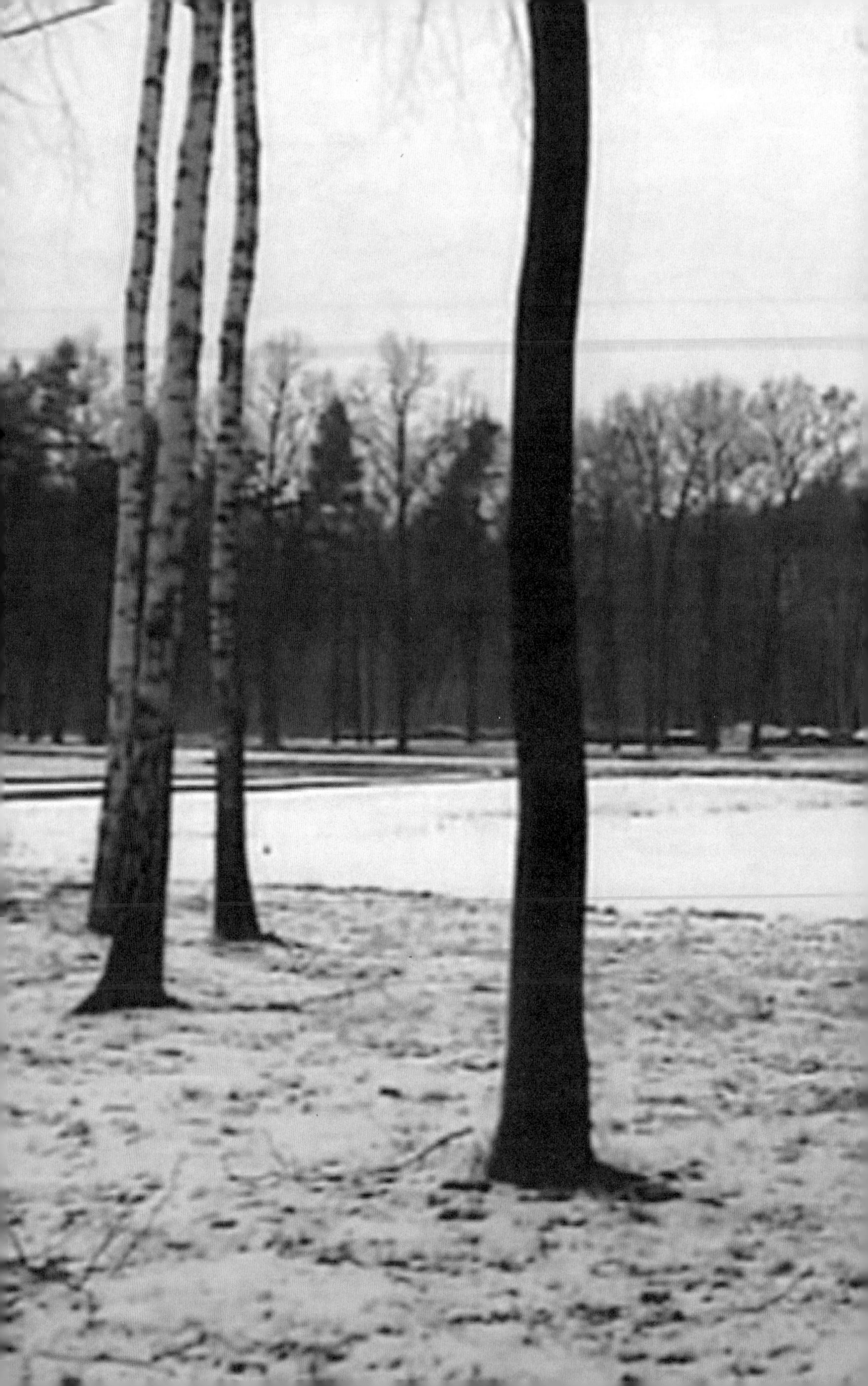

MIROSLAW BALKA'S GRAVES IN THE SKY

JAMES E. YOUNG

An unapologetic child of history, Miroslaw Balka came of age amidst the ruins and landscape of Polish national suffering. As the Polish landscape bore the literal, physical scars of World War II-era destruction and Holocaust, so too did Balka seem scarred inwardly by the memory of events he never knew directly. He carries within him the burden of a history that was not his making, the memory of a past that is being made constantly for him.

The grandson of a gravestone carver and the son of an engraver of tombstone inscriptions, Balka comes from a long line of monument-makers. But his medium is no longer stone; instead, it is the light, shadows and ambient sound of video-installation. Memory, in its ephemerality, demands an ephemeral medium. 'Every day I walk in the paths of the past,' Balka has said. 'Contemporary time does not exist. We cannot catch the continuous.'[1] How to reflect on this past without fixing it? How to grasp it without concretising it? We cannot catch the continuous, the artist implies, without making it discontinuous. As a medium, Balka's video-memorials are the closest the artist can come to gripping the ongoing, fluid presence of the past without fixing it. Like others in his post-war generation, Balka grew up to be a 'counter-memorialist' who bitterly rejects the memorial conventions that too often fix and thereby nullify living memory.

If the ruins of death camps such as Majdanek and Auschwitz-Birkenau are fixed in the landscape, the memory they generate in the artist is anything but fixed. In *Carrousel*, the barracks at Majdanek spin around us in a sickening swirl. The artist has trapped us in a memorial vortex, pulling us into the centre of the Appelplatz, the roll-call plaza, by the centripetal force of his spinning camera. Round and round and round the barracks whirl, a deadly 'Ring around the rosies, pocket full of posies, ashes, ashes, all fall down!' It is as if the Black Plague-era nursery rhyme and game were being set to a more recent mass death. Majdanek swirls around us as it spins unendingly inside the artist's mind.

Unlike *Carrousel*, which is installed vertically on the walls, several of his earlier 'video-memorials' based on the sites of former concentration camps have been cast horizontally onto the ground, grave-like. With their cinemagraphic illusion of depth, these video-gravestones seem carved into the ground, video-versions of negative-form monuments. For example, in his powerful video-memorial, *T. Turn* (2004), Balka has filmed the sky and trees while lying on his back near the ramp at Treblinka, waving his palm-sized video camera overhead in a quasi-circular trajectory, a double rotation that turns the tree-tops and fields into a spinning blur. The swirling landscape of sky and trees is projected onto the floor with the ambient sounds of a Hebrew-speaking tour-guide broadcast from above. Our eyes are drawn downward to the large horizontal square at our feet, covered in

coarse-grained salt to give the projected moving image a granular, stone-
like texture. But this is not fixed stone. Rather, gazing into this video-grave,
we see the sky, and we think of Balka's favourite poet, Paul Celan,
and his lines from 'Todesfuge':

> ... we shovel a grave in the sky
> there it won't feel too cramped ...

> he shouts scrape your strings darker you'll rise then
> in smoke to the sky
> you'll have a grave then in the clouds there it won't
> feel too cramped [2]

Balka's video-memorial is just this, 'a grave in the sky', the visual articulation
of Celan's brilliant poetic trope.

In two other, earlier concentration camp-based videos, Balka similarly turns
conventional memorial assumptions on their head. In *Bottom* (2003), also
installed on the ground, we stare down at the shaky, handheld video image
of showerheads inside the bath-house at Majdanek. The loud, echoing
footsteps of the videographer are piped in from above, the sounds of
our own hurried tour, our own escape from this concentration camp relic.
Endlessly looped, however, we are condemned to repeat our stampede
for the exit, for a way out, even as we can never leave.

In yet another, earlier camp-based video, *B* (2006), Balka has turned his
micro-lens onto the upside-down letter B in the infamous cast-iron slogan
'Arbeit macht frei' posted over the gate into Auschwitz-I. Through blowing
snow, this inverted B is accompanied by the ambient thunder of wind in the
microphone and the raucous laughter and joyful screams of young German
boys in a snowball fight, apparently taking place at the Gates of Hell.
The German voices and somewhat indecorous horseplay at the entrance
to Auschwitz make the site German again, reminding us that it was made by
Germans for largely Polish and Jewish prisoners. But by concentrating on
the inverted B, Balka does more than focus our thought on the resistance
of the camp-inmate and ironworker who, according to his diaries, sought
to sabotage the iron lettering. He also estranges the slogan itself and thus
breaks it down. Did 'Work make one free' at Auschwitz? No. And as it turns
out, neither does the artist's 'memory-work' make him free now.

In fact, quite the opposite. Balka is imprisoned by his memory-work.
It does not make him free, but rather it keeps his mind locked into the camp,
which he now carries within him, wherever he goes. Toward the end of
his heart-wrenching short-story collection based on his experiences as a
political prisoner in Auschwitz, the great Polish writer, Tadeusz Borowski,

observed: 'A certain young poet, a symbolic-realist, says with a flippant sarcasm that I have a concentration-camp mentality.'[3] That is, though liberated from Auschwitz, the writer was still trapped in the concentration camp of his mind. The world would now become his concentration camp.

It is this Holocaust-on-the-brain that turns otherwise small and banal objects of everyday life into ominous and threatening 'glints of evil' for Balka, and now for us, his audience. Thus viewed in *DB Real*, an otherwise pedestrian and inert Euro-pallet used for transporting dry cargo morphs into a haunting apparition of the inside of a cattle-car used by the Nazis to transport what they called Jewish 'Stuecke' (pieces) to the death-camps. The work's title, an acronym for Deutsche Bahn (German Railway), points in the direction of the artist's preoccupation. The grid of the pallet and blinking light behind it are suggestive of the small vents of the cattle-cars, the only source of light and air. It is all in the imagination, of course, evoked by very simple materials, their associations seared into the artist's mind, and now ours.

Similarly, in *AAA*+*Rauschsignale*, we share the artist's revulsion in the throaty roar of an internal combustion engine, producing nothing more than smoke and exhaust fumes, as it is revved continuously. With each rev, a spout of black smoke bursts upward into a steel-grey sky. A sustained rev will produce a little more exhaust. In this context, it is a killing smoke, of course, a smoke signal of mass death, a reminder of the exhaust used to kill victims of the 'death-vans' at Chelmno, and of the smoke of the crematorium chimneys. Lines from Celan's poem come again to mind:

> … you'll rise then as smoke to the sky
> you'll have a grave then in the clouds …

Are these smoke signals from history a terrible kind of code, or just the idling of an engine, spewing its exhaust to no other effect than to darken the heavens? Or did the heavens not darken, after all?

In earlier works, such as *BlueGasEyes* (2004), a single, long take of a round stove-top gas burner is named so that this simple, everyday object, too, is stigmatised. Together, *BlueGasEyes* become Aryan-blue eyes, and we're reminded yet again of lines from Celan's 'Todesfuge': 'Death is ein Meister aus Deutschland his eye is blue.'[4]

Balka finds his fragments of memory everywhere, even in others' films. In *Primitive* (2008), the artist lifts a 3-second excerpt from Claude Lanzmann's epic, nine-and-a-half-hour Holocaust documentary, *Shoah* (1985), thereby committing a benign larceny of a clip that was itself surreptitiously filmed by Lanzmann. In the excerpt, a former SS camp guard describes the primitive but deadly efficiency of killing at Treblinka. The guard, Franz Suchomel, has just said: 'Keep this in mind! Treblinka was a primitive but effective production line of death. Understand?' To which Lanzmann answers: 'Yes. But primitive?' Suchomel replies: 'Primitive, yes!' Primitive, yes!' This is looped endlessly, keeping it in our minds until it makes no more sense.

Of all his works, perhaps the *Flagellare* series is most fraught with violent portent. Projected onto beds of salt, the flinching, handheld video images of a shiny reflective concrete floor show three versions of a leather belt repeatedly, rhythmically and loudly striking its surface. With every sharp lash, the video image jerks a little, an inadvertent flinch of the videographer as he films and strikes at the same time, a twist on the notion of self-flagellation. The point of view is now the gallery visitor's own: what does it mean to whip with one hand and to record the whipping on film at the same moment with the other hand? In the cavernous space, the flagellation of the floor – one lash per second – sounds like a rifle-shot, each lash leaving its trace on the poured concrete floor, its sharp snap echoing in our ears.

At first glance, Balka's *Pond* seems to be a beautifully composed study in landscape: a small, still pond seen through the winter trees, with only the sounds of the wind, the videographer's even breath, the camera's whir, and a church bell ringing, or perhaps ringing children's voices. A rooster crows, the videographer breathes and the white birch trees are bereft of leaves. Birkenau is both a birch forest and a death camp. The wind in the microphone is thunderous and the breathing is soft, as if the artist is trying to still the slight quake in his hand. Like other post-war artists and writers, Balka is preoccupied by silence (nocturnal and divine) in the face of mass murder – and the impossibility of expressing such silence in any living, breathing memorial medium.

In *Bambi*, three deer are joined by one more as they graze in the snowy grass among the ruins of barracks at Auschwitz-Birkenau, all framed by barbed wire, fence posts and brick chimneys. The only sound is the wind in the microphone, as the deer run off through the camp, still enclosed by the barbed wire fence. The camera's telephoto lens collapses distance and the several layers of fences and barrack chimneys. The video is shot in colour, though in its winter tones it is largely monochromatic, except for the tan coats of the deer. All else is a study in black, white and grey, snow and barbed wire. Like the artist, the deer are trapped in the concentration camp, however whimsically and incongruously.

Mapping the Studio, Too and *Sundays Kill More* seem thematically out of place. *Mapping* is Balka's abbreviated homage to Bruce Nauman's original, *Mapping the Studio* (2001), itself an ironic homage to John Cage's famous silent movement (in Nauman's piece, a mouse breaks the stillness of a night-view of his studio). The shared preoccupation is the formal articulation of silence in space, shown in Balka's *Pond*.

Sundays Kill More seems a further conceptual stretch. It is set in a rainy landscape of distant trees, illuminated by flashes of lightening, accompanied by Charles Bukowski's recitation of his powerful poem of the same name. Is it possible that the artist would turn even Bukowski, the nihilistic, German-born American 'poet laureate of low-life' into a Holocaust poet? Probably not. Still, the mind reaches for associations: the Polish origins of the poet's name, the poet's attempted suicide by gas In 1961 (when this poem was first published), the poet's bitterness and bile: 'We're men, bitter, brave, and numb.' Is this what the artist hears in his brain while filming these landscapes? What happens when we view these works in the same space? Indeed what happens to us in the spaces between such works?

'My work doesn't occupy the whole exhibition space,' Balka has said. 'It occupies just a little bit of space, and the space that surrounds the work has the same importance as the space occupied by the object.'[5] That is, like other artists in his generation, Balka's installations leave space open not to be filled by viewers, but to open up space within viewers. The aim is not to crowd out the viewers' experiences with the artist's expressions, but to open space up for viewers' experiences of these expressions.

Like the other great counter-memorialists of his generation (Jochen Gerz, Horst Hoheisel, Micha Ullman, Renata Stih and Frieder Schnock), Balka sceptically critiques the redemptory premise of conventional memorials and monuments, the ways they can crowd out our own internal memory-work. Neither work nor memory- work actually makes us free. Every fixed memorial and museum carries within it the authoritarian logic it would have us commemorate, mandating how to think about the past, how to remember it. For lived memory, Balka suggests, look inwardly and outwardly at the same moment. By re-animating everyday objects of life in a landscape of ruins, the artist vivifies memory of the past with ongoing life itself.

1. Gregory Salzman, introduction to *Miroslaw Balka, Gravity*, University Gallery, University of Massachusetts Amherst, 2009, p.3.
2. Paul Celan, 'Deathfugue', trans. John Felstiner, *The New Republic*, 2 April 1984, p.28.
3. Tadeusz Borowski, *This Way for the Gas, Ladies and Gentlemen*, trans. Barbara Vedder, Penguin Books, New York and Middlesex, 1976, p.176.
4. Celan, op.cit.
5. 'Frogs, Knocks, and Other Blinks: A Conversation between Miroslaw Balka and Gregory Salzman on February 4, 2009' in *Miroslaw Balka, Gravity*, University Gallery, University of Massachusetts Amherst, 2009, p.14.

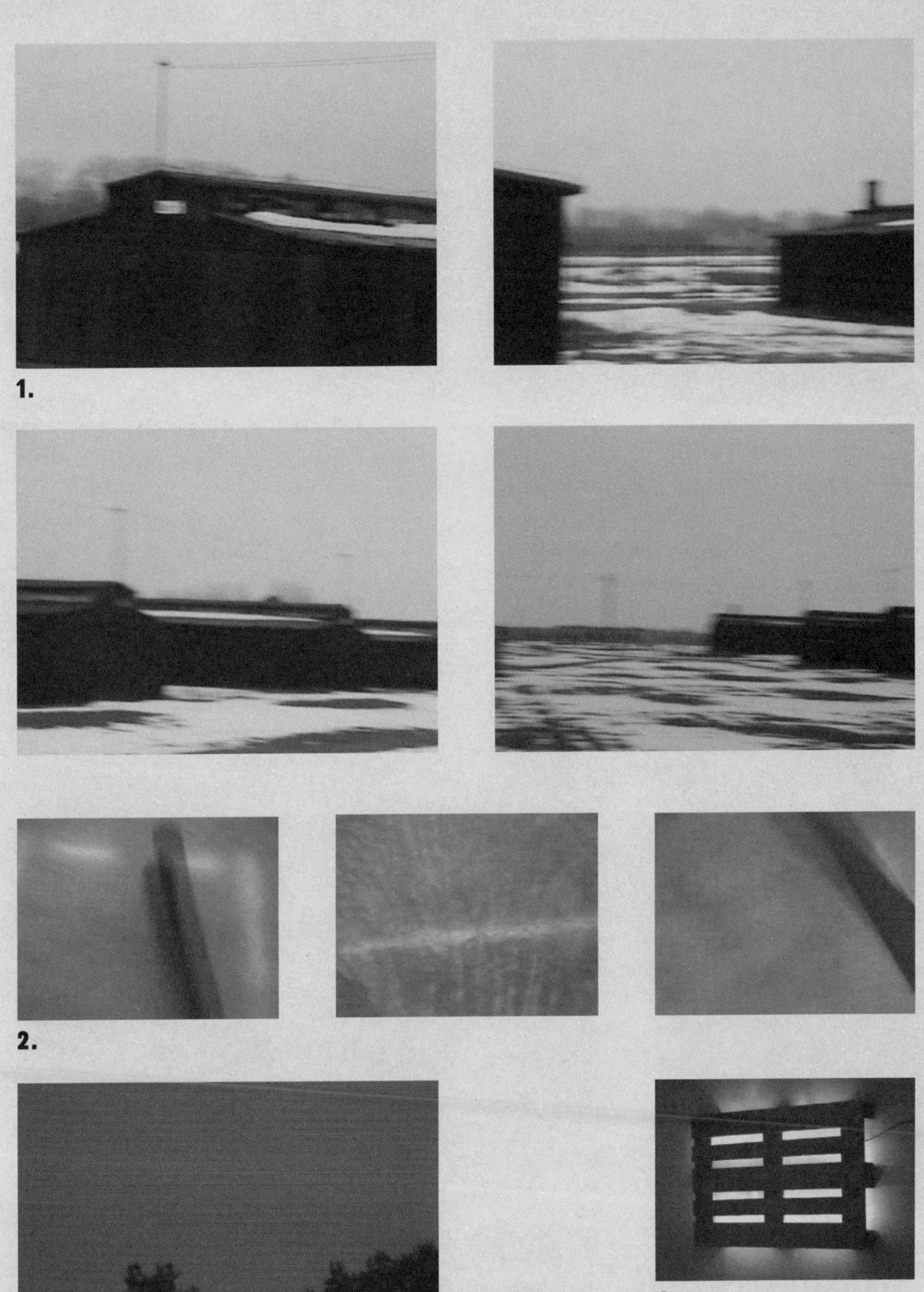

1.

2.

3.

4.

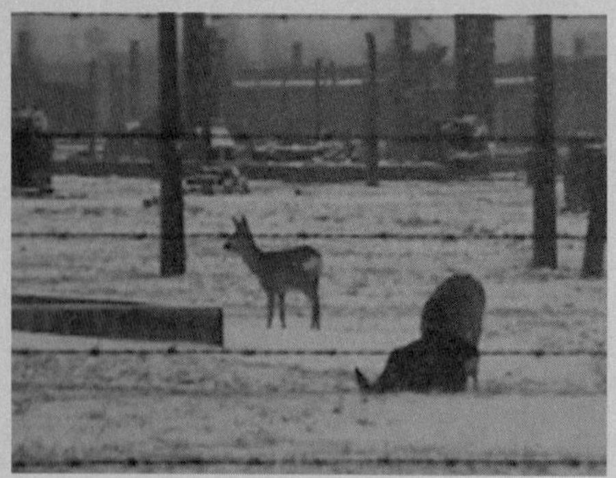

5.

6.

7.

8.

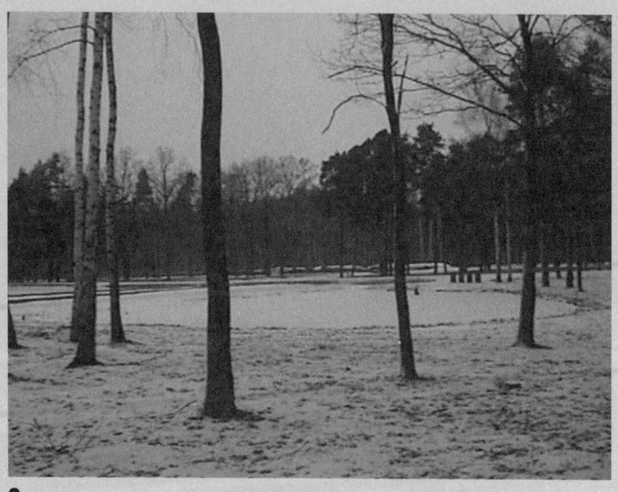

9.

1. *Carrousel*, 2004, video, steel, foam rubber, plywood. Courtesy the artist and White Cube, London
2. *Flagellare A, B, C*, 2009, video, steel, salt. Courtesy the artist and Gladstone Gallery, New York
3. *Sundays Kill More*, 2008, video. Courtesy the artist
4. *DB Real*, 2008, video, steel , salt. Courtesy the artist and White Cube, London
5. *Bambi (Winterreise)*, 2003, video. Courtesy the artist and Gladstone Gallery, New York
6. *AAA+Rauchsignale*, 2007, video. Courtesy the artist and Galleria Raffaella Cortese, Milan
7. *I Knew It Had 4 In It*, 2008, video, foam board. Courtesy the artist
8. *Mapping The Studio, Too*, 2008, video, steel, salt. Courtesy the artist and White Cube, London
9. *Pond (Winterreise)*, 2003, video. Courtesy the artist and Gladstone Gallery, New York

INTERNAL TIME / EXTERNAL TIME

SUZANNE COTTER

Miroslaw Balka is attracted to the non-spectacular, the discarded and the forgotten. His sculptures and installations are made from materials and objects, often found, and redolent with the memory of history and of individual and collective experience. Their indexical nature finds echo in his video works, in which registrations of light and dark record a particular place at a particular time. In their fleetingness and their evocativeness – wisps of smoke against the sky, the bored desperation of a man's voice, the repetitive motion of a wind-up toy in a darkened room – they are like the fabric of memory itself, a Proustian madeleine that, in provoking the act of recollection, affects us physically and emotionally.

Balka began making video recordings in 1998. The smallness of the recording equipment – a Sony handheld camera – and its portability meant that it could be secreted inside a coat pocket and provided him with a degree of spontaneity and discretion. The resulting, spare works are drawn from a hundred or so hours of recorded material. Consistent with his attraction to found materials and objects, the sites and situations that come under his scrutiny are rich in associative meaning. While the calamitous history of the Holocaust and the perpetuation of its memory are recurring themes, so too are broader reflections on life and death, survival and the human condition.

To interpret Balka's video works purely as exploring the limits of a sculptural practice that is widely renowned would be an oversimplification. A profound sculptural sensibility nevertheless informs how they are experienced. On a formal level, they extend a sculptural language of material, surface and scale with the tools of image capture and projection. As with his sculptural installations, Balka explores and exploits the limits of the medium, using it to literally shape the space in which it is presented. Projected onto the ceiling, the floor or the wall, his images are framed with physical constructions that serve as flat beds, eaves, or vertical supports. The visual and aural fabric of his images, too, are bound to the process and the place of their making, and resulting from a set of actions performed by the artist, be it climbing onto the roof of his studio to record the flashes of an electric storm, whipping the light reflections on a hard floor, or spinning himself around in the site of a former concentration camp.

His recordings are generally made at the beginning or the end of the day, or in the dark of night. People tend to be absent, or a peripheral blur, their voices forming a distant soundtrack. Sudden movements and shifts in and out of focus, combined with a mix of tonal ranges and light and dark contrasts, provide varying degrees of discomfort and disorientation. The multi-screen *Carrousel* is dizzying in its effect. Balka recorded its footage in the concentration camp of Majdanek, as he spun himself round in a circle while holding the camera outwards. The work consists of four projections of the same looped material, each set to a time delay of seconds relative to one another. The continual movement of the image and the loss of spatial referents that guarantee our orientation vertically in the world are nausea inducing. Barely audible sound and snatches of fragmented conversation add to the general feeling of disorientation. In the lower corner of one of the projections, a stencilled 'cut-out' of the Arabic-language news network, Al Jazeera, provides a further layer of coded information. The rapid scan of the surroundings includes the briefest of appearances of a group of people leaving the camp and conversing in Hebrew. Were we to recognise the language spoken, and the location from the sequence of frames that races across our view, we might reflect on the specific history of the camps, of the Shoah, of the transmission of news and of global conflict. Yet, even without this partial knowledge, we are presented with a palpable sense of lost time and its resident melancholy.

For Balka, it is less a question of medium than of means. He has described his working method as being like using a vacuum cleaner, hoovering up what is before him, taking it home and emptying the bag to see what is there.[1] The quality of the image and its editing are not at issue, rather, it is the decisions made and the processes involved in the image's realisation. The mechanism of the loop – generally between ten seconds and a few minutes – removes any sense of beginning and end point of traditional narrative, and serves to transform the fragment into a series of reiterations, an enveloping field of sensation, as unsettling as it is insistent. The choice of framing supports and the orientation of the video projection define the work as much as the accompanying sound – generally ambient, sometimes added, and captured at the same time as the video recording. We are made aware of our bodies, of our position, in a way not unlike the effect of encountering the corridors and walkways of Balka's sculptures – we hear the sounds of the wind, the crackling of footsteps on frozen earth or snow, people's voices, speaking Polish, German or Hebrew, coming towards us, moving away, the inhalations of breath close to our ears.

Balka's interest in the body is also 'an interest in the body that we create',[2] a reflection on the individual self in relation to the social order. In *Sundays Kill More*, flashes of lightening break across a murky darkness amid sounds of pelting rain and the laconic drawl of the German American poet, Charles Bukowski whose desolate picture phrases such as 'Sundays kill more men than bombs' strike the air as if into a spitoon of existential nothingness. *Mapping the Studio, Too* possesses the pathos of a Beckett play as we watch the image of wind-up mouse, spot lit by the camera as it mechanically scuttles across the floor of the artist's studio and is repeatedly stopped short by the wall only to begin again its futile circuit. In making *Flagellare A, B* and *C*, Balka used the belt from his trousers to subject his New York gallerist's floor to repeated blows. He describes his approach to making the

work as something like a primitive being trying to extinguish a source
of light. Projected onto a horizontal framed screen of salt, a perennial
material in Balka's sculptural repertoire, the gestures are violent and
persistent; their visceral thwacks against the polished concrete surface
physically unrelenting.

There is a strong relationship between the grounding literalness of Balka's
works and their poetic openness. Widely read, he is a noted admirer of
Joyce, Beckett and Celan. While the titles of individual sculpture works
are often reduced to empirical description of dimensions or the simplest
of designations, the naming of his many exhibitions takes the form of a
poetic construction of words and phrases in different languages alluding
to physical phenomena, places or no place in particular – *Lichtzwang, Jetzt,
Nothere, Gravity, Und Akupunktur, How It Is, Topography*. In the video
works, Balka seems to take this dual relationship further in a deliberate
confusion of the tangible world of things with what they might prompt
as reflections and response. In *AAA+Rauchsignale*, wisps of dark grey
smoke shoot up and waft across a less grey sky. Visually abstract, and
projected high above our heads, the work is at once allusive and porous
in its meaning. True to Balka's mining of personal memories in his work
and to his subtle sense of irony, the work's origins combine the themes of
a Polish lullaby (*aaa kotki dwa szarobure obydwa/Nic nie beda robily
tylko dziecko bawily* – 'Two little grey cats are taking care of you child'
) and a film about an Apache chief, Winnetou, which the artist recalled
from his youth. Recorded in a region of Croatia, used as the setting for the
original *Winnetou* film because of its perceived similarity to the landscape
of the American West, Balka asked a fireman to give a rendition of the
lullaby by using the accelerator pedal of his truck. In a play on the idea
of communicating through smoke signals, the resultant puffs of smoke
propelled into a sky of just over a decade-old wars offers an expression
of innocence turned to ash by violent acts, and of their memory dissipated
into the surrounding atmosphere.

Balka insists on the depth of curiosity that a work might provoke
depending on the degree of knowledge and experience of the person
encountering it. *DB Real* shows an urgently flashing light emanating from
beneath a latticed, wooden structure. The projection onto a framed screen
of salt placed horizontally on the floor reinforces the sense of doubling
at play (the work assumes an added, if not anecdotal, quality of the ersatz
in that the sculpture in the recording was unable to be transported to an
exhibition venue, prompting Balka to produce a portable video version).
The light source is, in fact, a Deutsche Bahn (German Railways) logo, the
title's eponymous 'DB', a name, Balka reminds us, that was in use at the time
of the transport of millions of people to their deaths in Nazi concentration
camps. For Balka, the meaning one might draw from the work depends

on the identity of the sign being hidden from view, its blinking presence serving as a metaphor for how tangible associations with the traumas of history can become embedded, if not lost, to a daily parlance of apparent innocence.

I Knew It Had 4 In It possesses a similar dynamic between physical and temporal layers and the space between looking and knowing. The motif, once again, is deceptively simple and chilling in its undertones. The title of the piece is taken from a segment of Claude Lanzmann's film, *Shoah* (1985), in which the wife of a former Nazi teacher at Chelmno concentration camp responds to the question of how many people were killed there – 4,000, 40,000 or the actual 400,000 who perished – with 'I knew it had 4 in it', as if remembering an item on a shopping list or the answer to a mathematical riddle. The recording of a figure of '4' taped in black against a white background is projected onto a horizontal screen filled with a similar support. The orientation is interchangeable from vertical to horizontal, from recognisable numeral to abstract composition of lines that zooms in and out of focus with the handheld movements of the camera, to the melancholic, synthesised tones of *The All of Everything* by Sun Ra. At moments compellingly ordinary in its clarity, it exerts a stifling pressure as the image becomes blurred and the dulled music threatens never to end.

Pond is hauntingly evocative. Projected on a scale close to that of the winter landscape it records, we see a snow-dusted pond in a small clearing of a forest in winter, the relative smoothness of the pond's contours surrounded by the slim, dark trunks of dormant birch trees, gently bowing like some brooding coven. Its pendant, *Bambi*, shows a group of deer foraging for food in the snow-covered grounds of a sinister-looking complex of buildings enclosed by barbed wire. The twitches and jolts to the camera, which offer fleeting glimpses of a broader field of view, serve only to increase the sense of unease. The deer themselves seem wary and, possibly alerted to the surveying gaze of the artist with his camera, pause and bound away.

While it is difficult to imagine a more stark and layered set of associations than those related to the history of the Holocaust and the genocide of millions of Jews on Polish soil, Balka defers to the power of suggestion rather than making explicit their identity or location. *Pond* and *Bambi* are part of what Balka has termed his 'National Geographic, come and see' approach. Both works, made in and around the concentration camp of Auschwitz-Birkenau, form part of a larger installation titled *Winterreise* (2003). The two videos were inspired by the music of Franz Schubert, writing as a young man about the loss of love, and Balka's own experience of the emblematic Eastern European landscape surrounding the camp and its tragic beauty, poignantly expressed by Holocaust survivor Shlomo Venezia in his book *Sonderkommando*, in which he describes his wonder at seeing the trees for the first time when he arrived at Birkenau.[3] Balka's response to this place of forests and deer and its dark history is a suite of brooding reflections on the morality of survival.

Writing about our constant exposure to images of war and trauma, and the ethics of looking at these images, Susan Sontag observed: 'To designate a hell is not, of course, to tell us anything about how to extract people from that hell, how to moderate hell's flames. Still, it seems good in itself to acknowledge, to have enlarged, one's sense of how much suffering caused by human wickedness there is in the world we share with others.'[4] Balka is engaged with this process of acknowledgement. He has talked about how the video camera allows him to assume the role of witness and to say something precise about his subject.[5] He presents himself neither as accuser nor defender but as the creator of a work of art that can carry within it the memory of past moments. If he is preoccupied with sites of history, not least the traumatic and yet to be reconciled history of his native Poland, his work insists on the present, a here and now that is collective but also specific to each of us. To the external time of our contemporary world, he brings to bear his personal subjectivity, the internal time of artistic expression. Exploring the limits not simply of a medium but of what is art, he gives form to sensibility from the fabric of simple and direct experience. If there is a harsh, unflinching reality to the video works, Balka's approach is one of both modesty and subtlety. He cares for the impressions he creates, he shelters them and contains such that they become one with the existing space as an enveloping sensorial field. He takes us beyond aesthetic contemplation to create a zone of immanence that is anything but transcendent in its anchoring in the here and now. Manifold histories, while concealed, buried or unacknowledged, remain necessarily of this moment. A new territory emerges. We are moved and we are mobilised.

1. Quoted from Adrian Searle, 'Miroslaw Balka on the ghosts of Treblinka', *The Guardian*, Wednesday 16 September 2009, Arts section, p.19.
2. 'Foot-Operated Boring Machine. Miroslaw Balka in conversation with Rafal Jakubowicz', *Pictokgram*, Year 7, 2007, p.96.
3. Shlomo Venezia, *Inside the Gas Chambers. Eight Months in the Sonderkommando of Auschwitz* (English Edition), Polity Press, Cambridge, 2009.
4. Susan Sontag, *Regarding the Pain of Others*, Picador, New York, 2003, p.114.
5. These and other observations come from conversations with the artist between February and October 2009.

MIROSLAW BALKA

Miroslaw Balka was born in 1958 in Warsaw, Poland. He graduated from the Academy of Fine Arts in Warsaw in 1985. Active in the fields of sculpture, drawing and video, he runs the Spatial Activities Studio at the Academy of Fine Arts in Poznan. He lives and works in Otwock and Warsaw.

Between 1985 and 2009, he had solo exhibitions at Pracownia Dziekanka, Warsaw; De Appel Foundation, Amsterdam; Galerie Nordenhake, Berlin; Galeria Foksal, Warsaw; Museum Haus Lange, Krefeld; The Renaissance Society, Chicago; 45th Venice Biennale, Venice; Van Abbemuseum, Eindhoven; Galeria Juana de Aizpuru, Madrid and Seville; Muzeum Sztuki, Lodz; The Lannan Foundation, Los Angeles; Le Creux de L'Enfer, Thiers; Moderna Galerija, Ljubliana; Tate Gallery, London; Museet for Samtidskunst, Oslo; IVAM, Valencia; Gladstone Gallery, New York; White Cube, London; The National Museum of Art, Osaka; Galeria Zacheta, Warsaw; SMAK, Gent; Kröller-Müller Museum, Otterlo; Museum of Contemporary Art, Zagreb; Dundee Contemporary Arts, Dundee; The Douglas Hyde Gallery, Dublin; Galeria Raffaella Cortese, Milan; Musee d'Art Moderne et Contemporain, Strasbourg; Arsenal, Bialystok; K21, Düsseldorf; Museum of Contemporary Art, Rijeka; Museo de Arte Moderna, Rio de Janeiro; Irish Museum of Modern Art, Dublin; Foundation Botin, Santander; WRO Art Center, Wroclaw; University of Massachusetts, Amherst; and Turbine Hall, Tate Modern, London.

Since 1990 he has exhibited in major international group exhibitions including: Metropolism, Martin Gropius Bau, Berlin; Possible Worlds, ICA and Serpentine Gallery, London; Documenta IX, Kassel; 9th and 15th Biennale of Sydney, Sydney; Rites of Passage, Tate Gallery, London; The Carnegie International 95, Carnegie Museum of Art, Pittsburgh; Distemper, Hirshhorn Museum, Washington DC; 24th Bienal de São Paulo, São Paulo; 1st Liverpool Biennial, Liverpool; Between Cinema and a Hard Place, Tate Modern, London; 44th, 50th and 51st Venice Biennale, Venice; SITE Santa Fe, Santa Fe.

From 1986 to 1989 he worked together with Marek Kijewski and Miroslaw Filonik as the Consciousness Neue Bieriemiennost. He has also worked in special exhibitions projects with Luc Tuymans, Rachel Whiteread, Doris Salcedo, Anish Kapoor, Antony Gormley, Robert Gober, Seamus Heaney and John Coplans.

JAMES E. YOUNG

James E. Young is Professor of English and Judaic Studies at the University of Massachusetts Amherst. He is the author of *At Memory's Edge: After-images of the Holocaust in Contemporary Art and Architecture* (Yale University Press, 2000), *The Texture of Memory* (Yale University Press, 1993), and *Writing and Rewriting The Holocaust* (Indiana University Press, 1988). He was curator of *The Art of Memory: Holocaust Memorials in History* (1994-95) an exhibition at the Jewish Museum in New York City, and editor of *The Art of Memory* (Prestel Verlag, 1994), the exhibition catalogue.

SUZANNE COTTER

Senior Curator at Modern Art Oxford between 2002 and 2009, Suzanne Cotter has curated over thirty major exhibitions and written extensively on contemporary art and artists.

TOPOGRAPHY
MIROSLAW BALKA

Published on the occasion of the exhibition:

MIROSLAW BALKA · TOPOGRAPHY
at Modern Art Oxford
12 December 2009 – 7 March 2010

Curated by Suzanne Cotter
Assisted by Emily Smith
Installation by David Garnett

Published by Modern Art Oxford
Editor: Suzanne Cotter
Editorial Assistant: Emily Smith
Copy Editor: Linda Schofield
Printed by: Petit Lublin, Lublin, Poland,
in an edition of 1,000
Design: Åbäke

Set in BLOCK

© Modern Art Oxford, the artist
and authors, 2009

All photography © Miroslaw Balka

Images courtesy of the artist, White Cube,
London, Gladstone Gallery, New York,
Galleria Raffaella Cortese, Milan

DISTRIBUTION IN UK & EUROPE
Cornerhouse Publications
70 Oxford Street
Manchester M1 5NH, UK
Tel: +44 (0) 161 2001503
publications@cornerhouse.org

ISBN 978-1-901352-41-2

ACKNOWLEDGEMENTS
Floriana Biundo, Alex Bradley,
Richard Calvocoressi, Raffaella Cortese,
Barbara Gladstone, Miciah Hussey,
Jay Jopling, Anna Mroczkowska,
Aneta Prasal-Wisniewska

MIROSLAW BALKA : TOPOGRAPHY is supported
by the Adam Mickiewicz Institute, Warsaw,
as part of POLSKA! YEAR and The Henry
Moore Foundation.

Modern Art Oxford
30 Pembroke Street
Oxford OX1 1BP, UK
Tel. +44 (0)1865 722733
www.modernartoxford.org.uk

DIRECTOR
Michael Stanley

STAFF
Allia Ali, Exhibition Organiser; Elizabeth
Berrett, Development Assistant; Erica
Burton, Art in Rose Hill Project Manager;
Sara Dewsbery, Press and Marketing Officer;
Sheridan Edward, Office Manager; Charlotte
Gretton, School Partnerships Coordinator;
Katie Harding, Head of Development;
Fiona Heathcote, Community & Education
Coordinator; Kirsty Kelso, Head of Marketing
& Audience Development; Sarah Mossop,
Head of Education; Barbara Naylor, Finance
Administrator; Barbara Retz, Café Manager;
Helen Shilton, Head of Operations and Visitor
Services; Donna Waterer, Operations and
Visitor Services Manager; Caroline Winnicott,
Head of Finance and Resources

COUNCIL OF MANAGEMENT
Chair: David Isaac
Hussein Barma, Jonathan Black, Christine
Butterfield, Roy Darke, Penelope Marcus,
Diana Parker, Amanda Poole, Navlika
Ramjee, David Reid, Robert Rickman,
Richard Wentworth

MODERN ART OXFORD

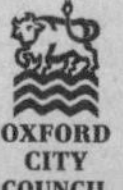

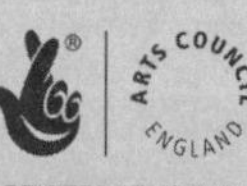

POLSKA! YEAR

Adam Mickiewicz Institute
CULTURE.PL

The Henry Moore
Foundation

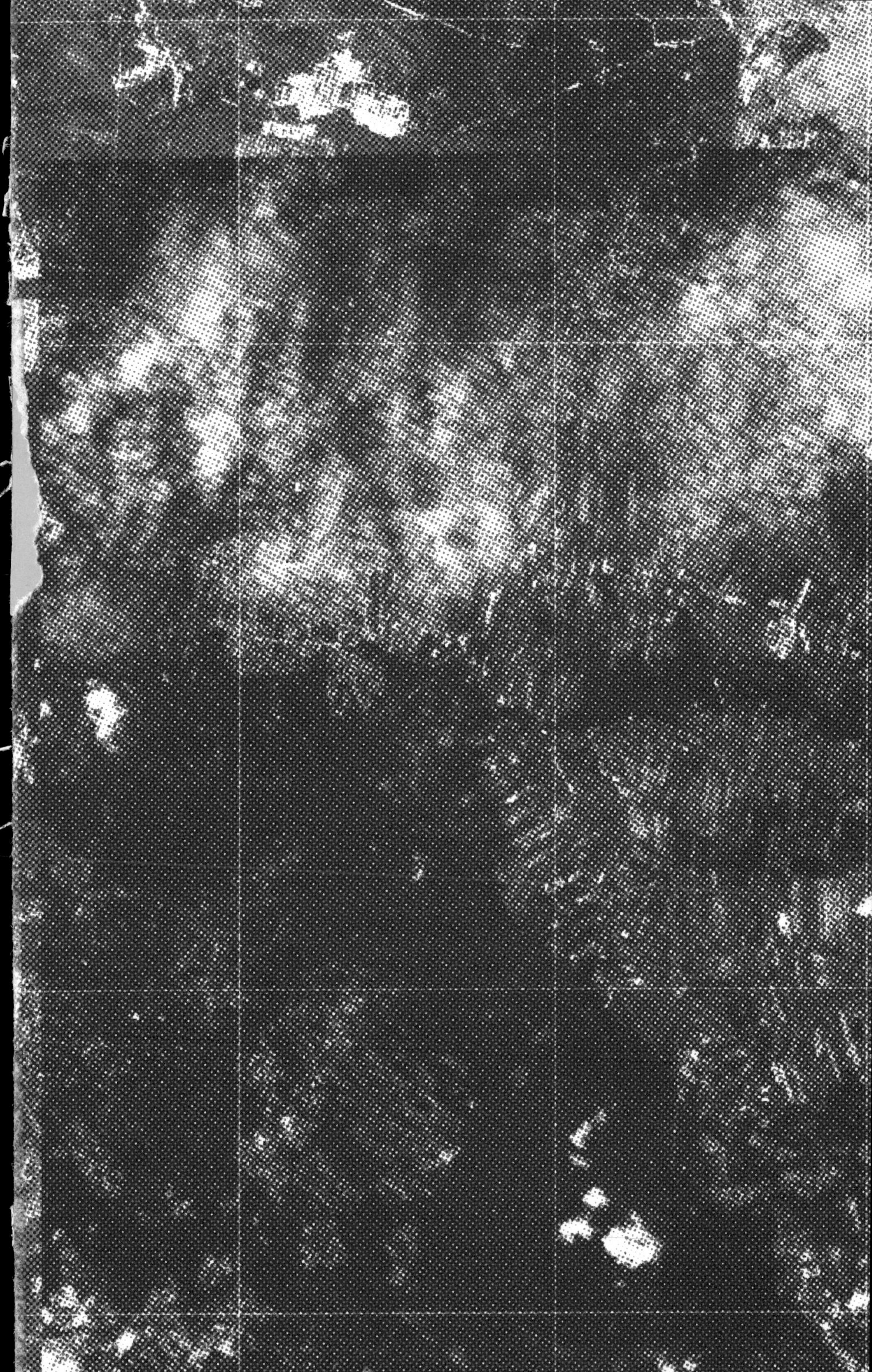

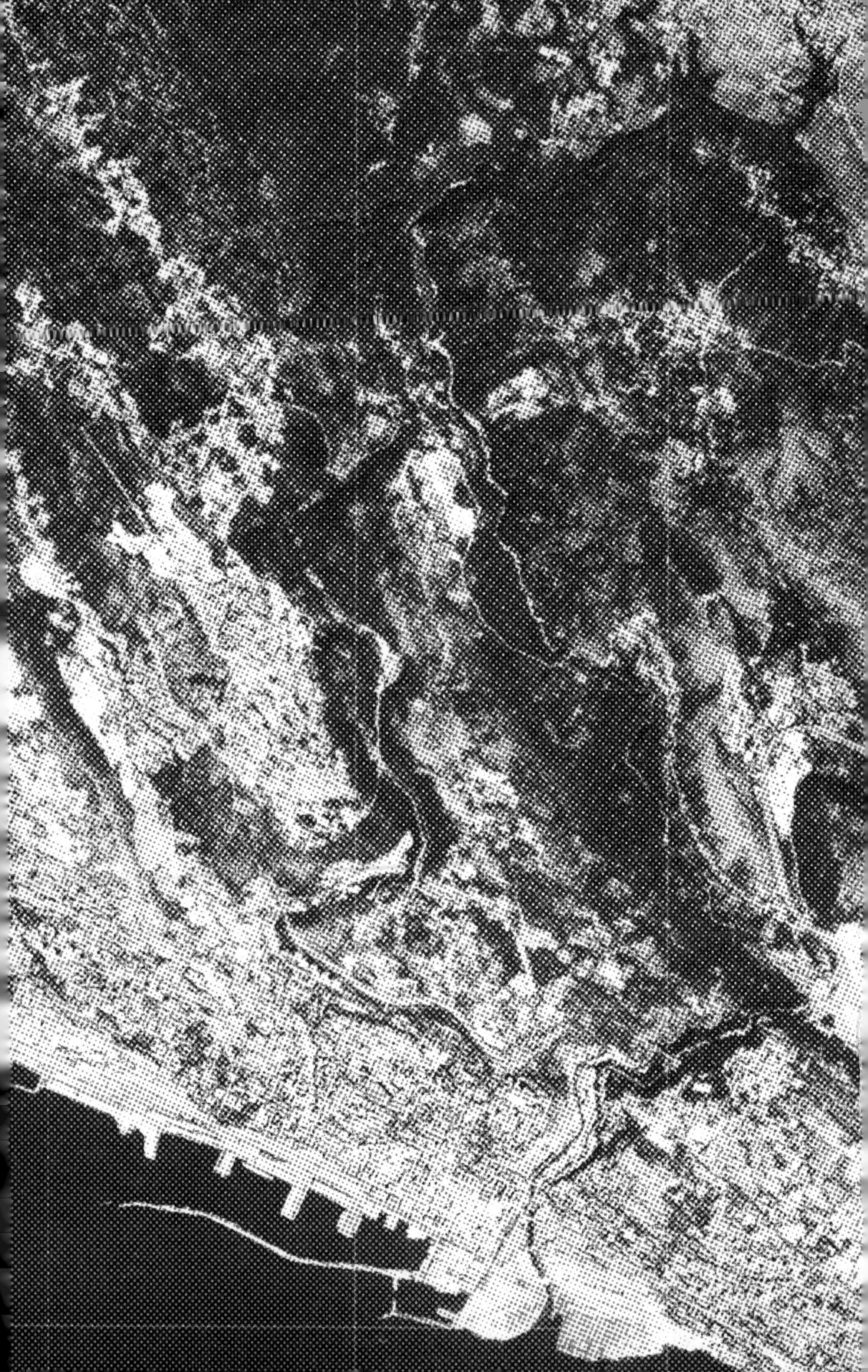